THE ANTI-HUSTLER'S HANDBOOK

A STEP-BY-STEP GUIDE FOR HARD-WORKING ENTREPRENEURS

Who Want To Redefine Success Now & Discover Infinite Choices for Fulfillment *Without* Sacrificing Everything That Matters

---

ALEX SCHLINSKY

Copyright ©2023 Alex Schlinsky. All Rights Reserved.

No part of this publication may be reproduced, distributed, or transmitted in any form or by any means, including photocopying, recording, or other electronic or mechanical methods, without the prior written permission of the publisher, except in the case of brief quotations embodied in reviews or certain other non-commercial uses permitted by copyright law.

ISBN: 9798392952045

Imprint: Independently published

Get the TOOLBOX

This book is designed to be actionable, and I've bundled all the resources that I've created for you into one easy-to-grab location.

Grab the companion tools from the toolbox and level up your results as you experience this book.

https://antihustlehandbook.com/toolbox

TABLE OF CONTENTS

Introduction 13

Preface 17

Part I: The Hustle 23

Avoiding The Freelancer's Trap 47

A Continuum 83

Part II: The Anti-Hustle 87

#01: A Victory Lap & Self-Assessment 91
    Take The ANTI-Hustle Self-Assessment 105

#02: Awareness & Recognition 115
    MINDSET 119
    ACTION 123
    TOOLS & RESOURCES 129
    REFRAME 131
    NEXT STEPS 133

#03: Focus & Prioritization 135
    MINDSET 141
    ACTION 143
    TOOLS & RESOURCES 151
    REFRAME 153
    NEXT STEPS 155

#04: Personal Relationships & Boundaries 157
- MINDSET 163
- ACTION 167
- TOOLS & RESOURCES 177
- REFRAME 179
- NEXT STEPS 181

#05: Professional Relationships & Profits 183
- MINDSET 189
- ACTION 195
- TOOLS & RESOURCES 203
- REFRAME 205
- NEXT STEPS 207

#06: Spending & Saving Money 209
- MINDSET 215
- ACTION 219
- TOOLS & RESOURCES 231
- REFRAME 233
- NEXT STEPS 235

#07: Team Management & Energy Preservation 237
- MINDSET 243
- ACTION 249
- TOOLS & RESOURCES 257
- REFRAME 259
- NEXT STEPS 261

#08: Present & Future Self-Accountability 263
- MINDSET 271
- ACTION 275
- TOOLS & RESOURCES 283
- REFRAME 285
- NEXT STEPS 287

#09: Growth & Change 289
- MINDSET 295
- ACTION 299
- TOOLS & RESOURCES 307
- REFRAME 309
- NEXT STEPS 311

#10: Balancing Now & Then: ANTI-Hustle Equilibrium 313
- MINDSET 319
- ACTION 325
- TOOLS & RESOURCES 329
- NEXT STEPS 331

ANTI-Hustle Toolkit 335

Recommended 341

Acknowledgements 343

About the Author 349

ΔΔΔ

"Entrepreneurs are the only ones that will work 80 hours a week to avoid working for someone for 40 hours a week"

- Lori Greiner

ΔΔΔ

Hustle Culture is OMNIPRESENT...

*"The dream is free;
the hustle is sold separately."*
— Marketers —

*"Hustle until you no longer need
to introduce yourself."*
— Ego —

"Hustle hard. Pray harder."
— Religion, The Hegemony —

*"Hustle isn't just working on the things you like.
It means doing the things you don't enjoy,
so you can do the things you love."*
— Business Culture, Entrepreneurs, Freelancers —

*"I'll rest when I'm dead. I've got a dream
that's worth more than my sleep."*
— Insomnia, Bad Habits —

*"Veni, Vidi, Volui, Vici" from the Latin...
"I came, I saw, I hustled*, I conquered."*
— Pretension —

"It's hustle and heart that will set you apart!"
— Coaches & Gurus, Comparison, Inadequacy —

ΔΔΔ

△△△

There is ANOTHER Way

△△△

INTRODUCTION

For ANTI-Hustlers, the goal of entrepreneurship is happiness and fulfillment — choice is truly the greatest gift of running your own business.

∆∆∆

The ANTI-Hustler's Guide

PART I Gets You Motivated...

If you need a connection to ditch the hustle and change your life, start with PART I: The Hustle. You'll find my ANTI-Hustle journey and what I learned along the way.

Be ready to **pick up practical tidbits, identify alternatives, learn to recognize red flags, and start seeing hustle culture for what it is.**

PART II Changes Your Life...

If you already know that hustle culture isn't right for you, then make a beeline for PART II: The ANTI-Hustle.

You'll do a quick and easy **personal assessment to identify your areas of need and match them to specific chapters to prioritize your time.**

Get a **plan and learn the specific action steps to take right now so you can start ANTI-Hustling today.**

Before You Go…

Any preconceived notions about ANTI-Hustle being synonymous with "not working" or even "not working hard" have to be stripped away right now because that ain't it.

We all know the layin' on the couch, get-rich-quick schemes that require zero work and even less effort don't pan out. Heard?

The problem isn't work or even hard work. The problem is that the hustle *lacks*. Exactly what does it lack? Plenty, but we can start with clarity.

"Hustle," to some, means "working hard and sacrificing for a clear goal" — *not the worst.* To so many others, hustle sounds a lot more like "working harder and faster and longer than everyone else in the room" because the "rent is always due" — not the best.

The problem with that kind of "hard work" is that it exists with no parameters, no defined beginning or end, and no boundaries.

The thing is, working hard **is essential**, but only within seasons of our life when we need it to achieve something tangible.

So, to us, that isn't the hustle; it's the *ANTI-Hustle* instead. Then, what's the flipping difference? Hustle will forever tell you, "There are no seasons except for one — hard work always."

Hustle is the unending season of 'work for the sake of working' persona, it's the 'if you're not growing your dying' attitude, it's the 'everyone is a competitor' mindset, it's the 'never stop, never settle — I'll sleep when I'm dead' living nightmare, it's the 'never bother to actually define what you want (*ANTI-Hustle*), because there's NO TIME — *JUST DO IT*' mentality, and it's just. not. worth it.

The colors don't change there. In truth, while there is definitely hard work to be had, you don't have to work hard indefinitely to be successful.

△△△

There is a BETTER Way

△△△

PREFACE

Hustling — ever heard of it?

It's thrown around in so many different contexts, that even pinning down a single agreed-upon definition is an unnecessarily hard and time-consuming challenge.

Most simply put, the hustle is allegedly about working hard and grinding it out to achieve ultimate success. And, only by going all in — the long hours, sacrifices, all the missed moments i.e. doing *whatever it takes* — will you finally get "the bag" that Mr. Broadus talks about so often, what you've deserved all along in the end.

Some people out there truly live and die by the hustle. For them — maybe for *you*, too — the hustle is the only way of life they know.

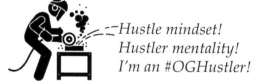

Hustle mindset!
Hustler mentality!
I'm an #OGHustler!

They're always grinding, always working, and always trying to get to that mythical sweet spot called "ahead."

And, for years, everyone has seemingly agreed that hustling is the only lighted path to success.

"Self-made" millionaires and billionaires swear by the idea that working harder and longer than anyone else is the basic approach to reaching even the easiest goals. *(But I'm not so sure they do.)*

They say it's all about grinding day in and day out to make your dreams a reality. *(But I'm not so sure it is.)*

But, what about **ANTI-Hustling** — "and just remember ALL CAPS when you spell the name" — ever heard of it?

In context with all the hustle culture claims, you probably already guessed that the ANTI-Hustle has something to do with the exact opposite of major hustle culture tenets. You're half right.

In its most basic form, the **ANTI-Hustle Model posits that the goal of entrepreneurship is happiness and freedom — time & financial freedom — and that choice is truly the greatest gift of running your own business.**

You should know that there's a promise of so, so much more.

This book is a step-by-step ANTI-Hustle Handbook with the information and the power to change your life, shift your mindset, and even build the foundations upon which to create successful 7- or even 8-figure businesses.

REAL big talk, right?

I come with first-person proof to back it up. Don't worry, I wouldn't have sent it to print if I didn't.

You should also know that you have options for how to approach the contents of this book and how to use the information to benefit you.

First, there's no wrong way to read this book, and it's **entirely up to you.**

After all, the real reason you became an entrepreneur was for freedom of choice, *right?*

(I mean, people aren't out there trading regular 9-5's for longer hours and a worse boss for *just anything*.)

But since it's still *my* book, I have a few very professional recommendations...

I thought you might start at the very first page of the book and read the whole thing, PART I: The Hustle & PART II: The ANTI-Hustle, love it, mark it up, go back to it, read it again and again, take pictures with it, frame it, read it one more time, display it prominently in your home or business.

Or, *whatever you think*, just so long as you start reading.

And, if you're a print person, I thought you might give it the honor of earning some coveted coffee rings and *gasp* maybe even fold over a corner or two as bookmarks.

Go right ahead! I love that!

Or don't — I know folding book corners is a polarizing practice. *No pressure.*

However, if you're already knee-deep in the business end of, well, your business and you need actionable steps to take — *like yesterday already, sir* — then make a beeline straight to PART II: The ANTI-Hustle.

From there, read PART II: Chapter 1.

This is the chapter that will outline how to find what you need in the second half of the book and how to best use what you find there to your advantage.

You'll also locate an assessment at the end of that first chapter to match your needs to certain chapters in order to help best prioritize what you need right now on your ANTI-Hustle journey.

After that, do what you will.

At that point, it's probably not quite yet time to display The ANTI-Hustler's Handbook prominently in your home or soon-to-be 7-Figure business, but you absolutely could.

You could also move to the next chapter and the next chapter after that to continue your progress.

If skipping around isn't your thing and you have a little time on your hands, you can also read this book in a more traditional, linear way, from front to back.

The trick will be to find what works for you and your business.

Hint: *That's what the ANTI-Hustle model is all about — redefining and achieving YOUR version of success FOR you.*

And no matter how you decide to approach the material, you'll walk away already having firmly planted the seeds of change in your life.

So, if you're an exhausted coach, consultant, freelancer, marketing agency, or other B2B/B2C service provider with BIG dreams and a packed schedule that overwhelms you more often than it pays the bills or pads your wallet, get ready to grow your mindset and your business.

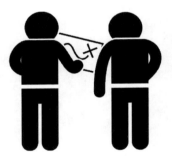

The ANTI-Hustler's Handbook will show you how to get from where you are right now to where you want to go with the tools and tactics you need along the way.

△△△

I can't wait for you to ANTI-Hustle your way to greater success.

— Alex Schlinsky

△△△

PART I
THE HUSTLE

> *My thing, my big deal, my "that one guy who does that one exceptional thing" is the 1-Call Close Sales Training.*

△△△

I've done it hundreds of times. I've sold millions of dollars worth of products and services. I handle objections. I have the right pitch ready. The framework gets sharper every day.

My team is trustworthy, and they have my back. I tell instead of ask on calls. I listen to build empathy and confidence in the prospect. The steps are clear and uninteresting, and no one gets confused.

The process is intuitive and transferable so that I can teach it to other people, and they can also make money.

I built it that way on purpose.

And it *works*!

Until it doesn't.

Before I get to the rollercoaster ride of my life, which ultimately brought *me* to the ANTI-Hustle lifestyle, I might as well begin with what you came here for:

What's the big secret to success in this industry? Ready for it? Want the truth?

If the funds aren't there — there is no close.

Say what?!

That's right. No funds mean no close.

There's no close, no matter how good you are.

There's no close, no matter how well you handle objections.

No matter how perfect your pitch is, there is no close.

No matter how great your framework is, there is no close.

There's no close, no matter how late you stay after or how early you get there.

There's no close, no matter how many birthdays you miss.

From the back, *What about financing?*

Ah, yes. The cautionary tale of financing. Financing means the funds are… **still not there.**

You know the client does not have the funds actually available. I know the client does not have the funds actually available. When we know this, and we just push through and squeeze water from the stone, it leads to predatory borrowing and lending practices.

You didn't think all the cautionary fine print was there just for fun, did you? It's there because little decisions just like this one have cost people far more than they originally financed — a lot.

This is a hustle ploy: to take advantage of every situation by squeezing everything they can, wrecking balls leaving nothing but ruin.

ANTI-Hustlers argue that it's important to minimize sacrifices and not destroy everything.

So, where's financing positioned?

If your potential client is looking at interest rates above 5% — no go. In fact, I'd say it's due diligence to advise them not just 'no-go' but 'never-go'.

The ANTI-Hustle doesn't support 'do'-ing on a whim. Making quick decisions (especially with high-interest rates) BEFORE you make a plan for how you will pay for them is a crisis lying in wait. **No. Go.**

That said, solopreneurs still growing and small businesses have taken advantage of smart financing to use essential funds to grow. What to do?

Stay the course of encouraging people to explore all the options they have for success, perhaps also point them to PART II: The ANTI-Hustle.

I'll repeat it.

If the funds aren't there — there is no close.

It's just that way sometimes.

If you peel away yet another layer, you'll discover that closing, otherwise known as success, won't always have the same definition.

I'm not just talking about lofty futures with a collection of Buggati Chirons, a permanent spot in Ibiza, or a full-service staff in three sovereign countries.

Plenty of rich people aren't successful — they're just rich.

Admittedly, being rich isn't the worst definition of success, but it is limiting. *Probably.*

So, figuring out what exactly success even means is the first seemingly impossible task.

The second outrageous task is the quest to find the lighted and favored path to get there.

(**Spoiler**: There isn't just one way, and looking for it is a major waste of your time).

The ambiguity in defining ultimate success makes the journey to achieving it unnecessarily long and incredibly hard.

Then, compounding the issue is what's left of a person and their life at the end of the journey. It is, well, actually it isn't always the picture of success anyone imagined.

In fact, there's such a mysterious disconnect between imagined success, the journey to achieve it, and what's left over at the end that it's a repeat plot line for countless books and movies — a Hero's Journey, anyone?

Let's agree that success can have different definitions. Infinite, even. Opposing, even.

... 36%, even?

ΔΔΔ

If we're not yet seeing eye-to-eye, that's okay — it's still early in the book. But, you have to be open to considering the possibility that there could be more than one version of success and there could be more than one way to achieve it.

So, let's talk about 36%. Sometimes you hit 36%, and you set the all-time high record in your entire industry, and sometimes you graze 36%, and you're as close to failing as you've ever been.

36% (0.366 to be exact) is the highest career batting average in Major League Baseball. *Ever.*

Ty Cobb, career-ending 1928, is still the record holder in MLB history.

I'm a football guy through and through (*Go Dolphins!*), but I can appreciate what the numbers here contribute to the larger conversation.

By MLB's standards, 36% is not just above average, but an all-time high, a record-breaking accomplishment. It's truly unmatched greatness at play for almost a century!

36% is also the maximum amount a household should spend of its monthly gross income on debt-related expenses. Hitting 36% or above by this measure is not an accomplishment. *Ever.*

THE HUSTLE | 29

If you surpass 36% by this standard, you probably won't qualify for the loan for whatever car *(likely not going to be a Bugatti Chiron — it's ok, me neither)* that you need to get to and from work reliably.

36% as a close rate on all the calls you book, also very surprisingly, scores well above average. You'd have to be smooth and, I mean, really smooth to get there.

For 36%, you would probably have a specific product or service that only you and your team could provide.

Your avatar would have to expertly match your messaging and marketing. You would already have a solid audience and likely a trademarked method to close the deal.

People would be sure that you are trustworthy in your niche.

With a closing percentage *like that*, you'd have to have it all and then some. Snap!

36% is, incidentally, a total bomb of a score on just about any standardized test. 36% isn't just an 'F', it's an 'F' for *real*.

 A 36% on an exam is a capital 'F' mega minus to the nth degree.

 When you get a grade like that, it's one of those where you thought you knew it, and then the grade came back, and you got everything wrong, but it was so bad that your teacher gave you mercy points just for writing your name kind of F.

What am I saying?

Success is highly negotiable at every turn. Whether you are successful now or if you become that way in the future depends first on the parameters by which you define it.

Why am I saying it?

You should not only judge success by standards that **Future You** will experience and enjoy down the road.

Be sure to remember to measure success by the standards that **Present You** can live with right now and appreciate along the way until you "make it big."

But isn't saying it always so much easier than doing it?

Is it weird that I find comfort and feel a little less guilty about the years I spent hustling so hard because when I first came to hustle culture, I came to it honestly?

△△△

'Aba' is a Hebrew word that's close to, but not an exact one-to-one translation for 'dad' — *it's so much more than that.*

Within the word itself are assurances of strength and obedience in the relationship; it means father, sir, thank you, and I love you in just those three letters. It also happens to be what we call my dad, *my Aba.*

So, you can guess I come from a pretty tight-knit family.

No surprise then that they instilled the value of hard work and ingenuity early in all of us.

Those ideals and values were standard practice for them. Before having kids, they were already hard-working, focused, and reliable.

When I was growing up, Aba was a funeral director; not the most lucrative profession, yet a vital one for our community. People knew him as a pillar of support for those grieving their loved ones — an essential and esteemed position.

Early on, I began to form the foundations for defining the success that I have today. I had plenty of my own thoughts and opinions about success, and even then, I had big questions about why things didn't always seem to add up.

I think I was maybe 10 or so when I asked, *"Aba, how come you're not as successful as [whomever]?"*

He stopped, put both hands on my shoulders, and ducked a little to look me right in the eyes.

He said, *"I am THE MOST successful man in the world. Because of you, because of your two brothers, because of your mother, because of the roof over our head, the food in our fridge, and our community who respects and appreciates our family. Success isn't about how much money you have in your bank account."*

Rock solid, right?

You just don't forget that kind of thing — it settles into a foundation for your thinking and doing. At least, I haven't let go of it yet, and I hope you'll hold on to it, too.

Still, after years of being successful, he shifted gears to find a way out of the funeral business. The stress compounded with all the grief and emotions from funeral services compelled him to move to something new. It was actually my mother who inspired Aba's entrepreneurial journey with her own.

She had been with Jessica McClintock for years — reach way back for that one. She was incredibly successful there but then decided to pursue a different venture.

She went after an entrepreneurial dream that combined running a business, personal fulfillment, and her true passion, art.

With that, she became incredibly successful. Planning her next move and becoming an entrepreneur was a fantastic choice for my mother.

An artrepreneur? *Is that a thing?* If that's a thing, my mom is definitely a top-tier artrepreneur.

She created an after-school program for kids of all ages. Kids as young as four years old to aspiring teenage artists would find a way to connect with art, thanks to my mom.

There was real magic in the way she could communicate her own love of creativity in such a way that made everyone else feel perfectly comfortable sharing too. That's an amazing gift — as if being a crazy talented artist wasn't enough!

mom's actual art

That's how *she* served the community. In those ten-plus years, she sustained two art studios where she taught classes and combined her love of creating and teaching.

Her art is amazing, and her work within the community is universally beloved.

Aba loved how her choices topped her fulfillment levels. Her entrepreneurial vision and purpose not only inspired plenty of young artists but also my dad to step out on his own.

He walked away from his longtime position as funeral director when I was just a pre-teen. He wanted to continue to help the community but in a different way.

After some thought and a little more inspiration, his answer was a financial planning start-up.

From nothing, he worked to build his own company. In just a few years, he amassed a healthy roster of clients and was really making it.

Business was booming!

As a kid, it seemed "booming" to me. His choice to switch careers really benefited my family financially. Even a young kid like me could see that much pretty plainly.

My older brothers were in college, and I attended a top school in the area. We had the money and most importantly the time for everyone to go on vacations together.

We had enough so Mom could retire early, and she did. The new business had opened up financial opportunities that weren't there for us before.

Everything was great!

During those years, I felt like we were very much on top of everything — the world, the game, the moon, the list, the line, and spaghetti… on *top of it all*.

If you asked me to define "success," pretty much everything about my life at that time would have been the fast answer.

And I would have been *so sure.*

But there were things I didn't know then. Now, those same things I know all too well. Looking back, it's clear that I had no idea what was happening.

Like, none — *complete* goose egg status.

I didn't realize how pouring 100% of yourself, 100% of the time into your career robs you — whether or not it's your business. I didn't know the full impact of grief, stress, and trauma.

And, loss was entirely lost on me.

I didn't know about the ways in which a funeral director position could affect a person, especially not someone as strong as MY Aba.

I had not yet embarked on entrepreneurship or the days of work followed by the evenings of painfully making time to "show up" — **if** you can count it as that — for your family only to then head back to the nights of work that then blur to the next day and again and again and again.

And running a business?! Ha! I thought about it like a game, the same as Monopoly.

When you make a certain move, another move follows — someone else's turn, and nothing bad ever *really* happens.

So what if you lose colored paper money or plastic playing pieces?

I didn't understand that very real and very big losses come with the potential for actual gains.

Not yet, I didn't.

Then, Aba had a major debilitating stroke.

People who have been in shock before will know this setup — there's just one way to describe all the events that happen right before, during, and after a traumatic event. Time stands still.

△△△

I still know exactly where I was — in my bedroom. I still know exactly what I was doing — playing GameCube. I still remember exactly what he said when he walked through the door…

> "We need to go to the hospital right now. I can't feel the left half of my body."

… and the car ride to the hospital is still a slow-motion dream sequence for me. It wins for the longest car ride in total silence and in total disbelief. I'm not sure anyone, including Aba, believed what was happening.

△△△

He was only 47. I didn't understand. My own personal Superman was supposed to be invincible. He exercised regularly, ate well, and always went to work for his family — everything a person is supposed to do.

How could this happen to a person who does and has always done everything they are supposed to do? I couldn't wrap my head around it at 15, and my father hadn't planned for it at 47.

An aneurysm caused his stroke, and all the events that followed changed my family's and my life's trajectory forever.

It's just that way sometimes.

The most important thing for all of us is that Aba survived. That's what counts — the big win.

∆∆∆

Everything else? *Not so much a big win.*

The short and long-term prognoses were devastating for him *and us*. And not just medically — everything else was in critical condition, too.

For me, it was terrifying just to consider what could happen next.

I spent night after night wondering if he would even be the same person. I panicked. It scared me to think about a stranger coming home in place of my dad. Would he even still know me? Would I even still have a dad if he doesn't know he has a son?

Meanwhile, the medical bills that were already astronomical from his emergency room bills were still growing to treat his ongoing needs.

Then, even more problems developed because of complications from the initial stroke. We experienced shockwave after shockwave that continued to affect him medically and all of us financially well down the road.

The hits just kept coming and coming.

The income from his financial planning business would have been a lifesaver during this time.

Unfortunately, we learned it was totally inaccessible unless he was the one there to run the show. The business was useless without him at the helm – dead in the water.

Though understanding and kind, the clients couldn't wait forever, and they didn't.

We tried our best to keep it all together, but everything to run the business was inside my dad's head — that vault was locked up tight. No one had access to keep the company afloat.

And then, the business my dad worked so hard for turned out to be just a freelance operation that effectively stopped in its tracks the moment my dad had the aneurysm.

It shuttered on his inability to maintain operations because the information wasn't readily transferable. He had no systems in place or procedures outlined that would make stepping in and running the business possible, even in just an emergency capacity.

My mother, who had just retired, tried to return to work as quickly as possible. That wasn't enough either.

And then, all that we had grown accustomed to was gone.

She was doing what she could to continue to pay bills while trying to hold it together for all of us. The money just wasn't there to save the house where my parents raised us.

And then, the house we became a family in was gone, too.

Once our house sold, it seemed like anything could go up on the chopping block. What was next? What else could we possibly lose?

△△△

Instead of just hoping for the best and relying on friends and family, we eventually decided we had to do the old 'hustle harder than all the rest.'

Our new goal was to do anything we could to make it work.

We weren't always sure what "it" was, but we knew we had to do whatever that was as quickly as possible — **and this is hustle culture at its core.**

Until then, I had only really seen two approaches to working hard. There was the solemn and no-nonsense entrepreneurial pursuit from when I observed my dad start his business as a financial planner.

Then there was the hard work mixed with the joy of following and developing your passion I learned from my mom's entrepreneurial work.

I always knew it all took a lot of effort, work, focus, and energy to start a business, but I also assumed it always paid off.

I had just learned that it only pays off *until it doesn't.* The urgency of the real and deep entrepreneurial hustle culture had now set in for me, and all of us.

We had to work hard and fast. Then harder and faster, to make something else better happen, or something worse would surely happen instead.

The ideology of the approach we took is also, and you might have picked it up already, another central tenet of the **1-Call Close.**

You don't close successfully by just highlighting what they stand to gain...

You close successfully by making sure they know exactly what they stand to lose.

They say that near-death experiences are often the catalyst for extraordinary change. I know that my dad's stroke and the following events changed everything for me, and for all of us.

[Third-Person Omniscient Narrator Hot Take:]
Little did Alex know, he would still have so many more shocking revelations, unfortunate events, missed core memories, dodged opportunities, WTF moments, industry clichés, confusing untruths, and unfulfilling experiences that would all amount to just more drops in a big bucket of endless breaking points on his long, hard-knock journey before finally embracing the ANTI-Hustler ideology.

△△△

When Aba suffered a stroke from a major aneurysm, everything was touch and go, but thankfully we didn't lose him then.

What we did lose was our financial stability. He was out of work and in recovery for years.

And that sh!t *sucked*. Big time. Welcome to Sucktacular City, Population: us.

The good news is that, eventually, Aba bounced back and into a success greater than even before the stroke.

After his recovery, and with some serious reflection, we both have come to some insightful conclusions — his always far greater than mine.

Aba figured out the problem, found several practical and translatable solutions, and made it his work to help other people avoid the same nightmare.

He reopened a successful financial planning *business* — this time an actual business with systems, processes, revenue, and stability.

Aba also went on to share his knowledge by teaching seminars on the experience, its immediate and lasting impacts, and how to avoid it.

Don't just take my word for it, though.

He's got a book out there that is so worth your time. I hope you feel as lucky as I do that Aba got to write the book and that I got to read it.

The ANTI-Hustle
Avoiding The Freelancer's Trap

△△△

For a business to be truly successful, it has to be equipped to run without the owner.

If the business cannot run without the owner being present for daily business operations, it has effectively fallen prey to *The Freelancer's Trap.*

While it's true the greatest thing about freelancing is working when you want, one of the absolute worst things about freelancing is also that you work when you want.

It is so very difficult to implement effective systems and processes when you're always scrambling to hustle your next deal.

Scrambling aside, very few entrepreneurs just starting out have an actual detailed business plan, clear goals, or milestones to hit that goal, let alone all the systems and processes required to delegate the workload to be successful long term.

This is too common!

By not making systems and processes a priority, you make your business more vulnerable to collapse instead.

One major mishap goes down, and it's time for you to close the shutters for good. #Facts.

Aba knows it. I know it. In fact, plenty of people know it all too well — *too many*.

It's typical hustle trickery untruths at play again.

You can call it a business all day long, but in reality, you can't pull a business out of your — ahem — *hat* when you haven't done the necessary foundational work.

And it IS necessary. It's essential, it's crucial, and it will end up being the make or break for your business in the end.

Otherwise, you're still freelancing just to make a quick buck over and over again.

The forever pursuit of a quick buck has taken the steam out of a lot of good ideas and businesses, and people.

It's not sustainable.

Take it from Admiral Ackbar — **"It's a trap."**
(Where my Star Wars fans at?)

It also might shock you that **businesses rarely recognize they're in The Freelancer's Trap.**

In fact, some business owners "know" their business is so fully fleshed out and successful that they are ready to scale instead.

In actuality, it should be the complete opposite.

When I consult with businesses unknowingly caught in The Freelancer's Trap, like Aba was, I try to be as frank as possible.

More often than not, I recommend that if they do scale, it should first be right back down to re-establish the right systems and processes.

Clarity changes everything.

Foundations have to come first.

The in-between is a dangerous place to be for anyone... *for everyone.*

Half-drawn game plans will effectively force you to hustle on and on, indefinitely.

Sure, that's great for the hustle, but not so great for you.

The ongoing impact will directly affect longevity, your own ANTI-Hustle journey, and the long-term success of both Present and Future you.

If you have employees, remember that you provide them with financial stability in return for their commitment to the job. They're counting on you.

You took on that responsibility when you hired them.

No matter the fine print, roles, or jargon of contractual terms, be sure to carefully mind the human terms first — be human first.

In due diligence, take the time and effort to evaluate the current state of your business, what needs to happen, and how to get it done for everyone's sake.

Pssst. You should start *right now* and *you can.*

You need to find out what is currently happening in your business, and then act purposefully. Determine what needs to happen right now to be more successful, and then map it out so that everything works out okay later, too.

Most importantly, don't forget to plan out how to get it done before you make more moves.

A word of caution: **Keep a close eye out for hustle culture.**

The hustle will sabotage planning every single time in favor of chaos, always in favor of 'waiting until next time' over reaching a resolution.

The hard truth is that it's likely still impacting how you do you.

Oh, you thought you quit all that when you resigned from your job and opened your business or this book and became your own boss?

Not so fast… despite your best efforts, the hustle can creep back in.

Hustle culture is so slick and so sly. It always has been and always will be. It's the OG "snake oil salesman." It's as intoxicating as it is deceptive.

Even if your hustle game is strong, you might not be as spirited as you were when you started.

But, make no mistake, the hustle is still as strong as ever.

And, if you've been in the business, any business, even if for just a few weeks or months, you are probably at or reaching the first of many breaking points.

And, no, it doesn't matter whether or not you're willing to admit it to yourself — *the hustle knows*.

It's just that way sometimes.

It could happen to anyone, and I know it does, but that's how it happened to me.

△△△

[Alex:] Hi, I'm Alex, and that's how MY toxic relationship with hustle culture started.

[Group:] Hi, Alex.

△△△

I really try to make sense of sticking so hard to hustle culture for so long. Every time though, it gets a little dicey for me at the point when Aba finally bounces back.

Yet, even then, even when he had come around full circle and was back at it, and everyone was comfortable, there I was — still entrenched in the hustle. I still *"had to"* do it.

Investing so hard into hustle culture gets even shakier on my end when I finally get my own businesses in order and stop writing $1 articles and start making 6-figures.

Right? But, wrong. Even still, I remained stuck in the hustle.

"Can't stop the hustle, baby!" Ugh.

The truth is, and it's not really a spoiler because the real story here is to make sure that yours turns out better than mine, is that I actually don't end up parting ways with hustle culture until after a few more long years and a significant crisis of my own.

The whole time, it always seemed so "necessary" and so much an integral part of my "success."

For me, there was *no other option* but to hustle. I had to hustle, right? Have you heard my origin story — *it's tragic!*

So, I get it if you still feel the very same way right now. I do.

For you, it might still feel very necessary, very essential, and very much the only option available.

But know this: everything you want that you're so sure can only be achieved through hustling can absolutely be achieved through ANTI-Hustle.

Where you are is a tough spot to be in — it is. And you might not believe me just yet, but by the end of our time together, the ANTI-Hustle will be a very real possibility and just one of the many new choices you have!

I'll be there.

I can't wait for you to see the light at the end of the tunnel — it's such a pivotal moment.

Until then, I'm sorry to report that you likely have a few hard knocks to get through first.

And I would know.

> *Don't misunderstand — just because it could happen to anyone doesn't mean it's not still really, really hard.*

∆∆∆

Contrary to popular belief, you actually don't need to have a tragic, uplifting, or moving backstory to enter the hustle.

There aren't any requirements, really. It's there and open for business 24/7.

The 24/7 part IS mandatory, though, because the hustle never stops. Never.

I mean, you DO want to be *successful*, don't you?

You don't want to be a *failure*, right?

Thanks to the giant, churning hustle machine, we are constantly being told to work harder and faster if we want to be successful.

Hustle culture pokes and prods with shame and guilt to do more and more and more.

There is no end.

But what if you did stop?

What if we all stopped and took a moment just to slow down and take stock of our own actual situation right now?

Stay with me, what if you just... didn't hustle?

Whoah! Wait a minute!

Before you close the app or shut the book, pissed off and *just* so *eff-ing* tired of lazy, life-hacking, viral quiet-quitting nonsense — I'm bringing something else to the table.

By the way, *objection handling* is what that last bit was, you know? It's super formulaic.

Keep in mind that, even though it has a structure, it's important to just use it as a framework rather than a set script.

The more natural each conversation is, the better.

Here's the setup:

You have a problem and/or a goal, and I want to help (using the product or services I'm trying to solve your problem with).

You might be apprehensive about what I'm suggesting or going to suggest.

I'm already in the know about some potential apprehension you might have. I'm prepped and ready.

What? How?

I already know my offer is a little different from the norm.

So, I quickly address your potential objection with my recommended method as a natural part of the conversation before you have to ask.

As a result, you get the answers you need and feel heard and more at ease.

Now, we can move forward — *together*. When we're in it together, that's where the real magic can happen.

If you're here thanks to my work with the **1-Call Close**, you know that objection handling is a crucial part of that process.

By the way, that whole process ISN'T just me, objection handling is an essential part of any sales situation.

So much so, I address it at every conference and summit and engagement and convention and forum and, and, and...

I also offer a cool $100 to anyone that can come up with an objection that I can't successfully handle — that IS just me.

To date, no one but yours truly is $100 richer.

Open invitation: please change that.

So, I hear your objections. I *really* do. I'm betting they sound something like this:

- But isn't hustling just part of it? No one ever got anywhere good without working hard!
- Don't I NEED a "side hustle" outside of my **main** hustle on top of my job to be successful? It's an average of 7 streams for millionaires, right?
- If I don't hustle, won't that make me a *failure*?
- Look, hard work never hurt anyone — I'm so *tired* of this false narrative where people think they can be successful without hard work.
- Isn't the entrepreneurial spirit built on brow sweat and elbow grease, long days and sleepless nights, refusing invites to parties, receptions, birthdays, and promotions, and taking the lonely road and burning the candle at both ends with the midnight oil at the same time?

Does any of that nonsense sound familiar to you?

It sure does to me.

That's just an iota of what hustle culture convinced me to believe as it *robbed me blind* for the years and moments of my life — all under the guise of "things to do necessary for success."

To that line of "reasoning," I will always and forever wonder:

- What is it you are hustling so hard for?
- Why do you want it so bad that you would give up so much for so long?
- When do you expect to get it finally, that thing you "deserve"?

You should absolutely wonder the same, but the objections aren't entirely misguided.

There are a lot of things people try to sneak past you as "good old fashioned hard work" that is "absolutely" necessary "100% of the time" to be "successful".

I challenge that assumption.

How come?

Hustling has long been considered the ultimate key to success — the norm if you will.

To that end, entrepreneurs especially are almost bullied into hustle culture buy-in from the very beginning of their tenure, be it long or short.

It wasn't ever news to me, and I'm sure it won't be news to you, that constantly pushing yourself to and past the limit will eventually lead to burnout, health problems, strained relationship, poor impulse control, clouded decision-making, and everyone's favorite — decreased productivity.

Would you hire someone with such shining promises of outcomes and key results?

I hope the answer is 'no' — it's just not good business.

So if you're in the thick of it, having "clouded decision-making" means you might not be able to see the forest for the trees.

Not recognizing non-stop hustling to no end can be incredibly harmful.

So, please, no matter where you think you are on the hustle spectrum or on your own ANTI-Hustle journey, pause and take stock.

Just by clearly defining and maybe redefining a few key elements, you might be surprised to find that you can still be successful *without* the damaging parts central to the hustle.

It's past time for you to stop hustling so hard.

But the concept might seem out of reach right now if you haven't before considered any other possibilities.

So, let's do that.

Right here. Right now.

We can run through the possibility together, so you'll know that you're not the only one who struggles with the idea of the *F-word* (no, not that f-word, but they do usually travel together).

THE F-word ... failure.

If failure is the first thing that crossed your mind as something that could happen if you stop hustling, you're right!

That's correct — failure is a viable option.

But, it's also only a detractor if you're still afraid of failure.

But, you're going to have to move past that, eventually.

It's the same *"hustle hella hard, never celebrate a holiday"* mentality that will likely end up being the very thing holding you back from the "later" you've been hustling for the whole time.

It's just that way sometimes.

In Hustle Culture, there is ALWAYS more — do more, get more, be more, and have more. But if the hustle hinges on the idea of a promise in a future where it all finally pays off, what happens when the magic hourglass breaks?

△△△

If you thought one near-death experience wasn't enough to really drive home the heaviness of hustle culture, don't worry, fam — *I got you.*

After Aba had his stroke, I was inspired and terrified. Enough so that I was determined to do whatever it took to make "it" happen for me.

By "it," I honestly meant the super-successful part where I learned from his mistake and went on to make money and enjoy life, but...

When I was 14, we almost lost my dad.

When I was 18, I almost lost my life.

All dramatization aside, the truth is this: when I was 18, I learned that I was living with a life-altering heart condition that would require surgery.

I found out that I was born with a bicuspid aortic valve — your standard textbook congenital heart defect. Classic!

The "defect" part is that blood leaks back into my heart. As a result, the size of my heart will continue to increase over time, just like any muscle would when it's overworked.

Except, this kind of gain is the one that gets you early-bird access to an obituary, not one that gets you to the top of the leaderboard at your local gym.

The doctors said,

> *Alex, you'll need surgery, no doubt.*
>
> *The good news is, you won't need it for another 20-30 years. By that time, the medical advancements will be astounding.*
>
> *It's not something to worry about.*
>
> *Go on and live your life.*
>
> *You have time.*

Admittedly, this was not the greatest news.

I had BIG plans laid out, and I was looking toward the future as the promised land. In no far away dream of success was there an open heart surgery chapter.

Thankfully, I was 18. There aren't a lot of opportunities to look back and be thankful for being 18, but this is one.

At 18, even the worst things have a way of sounding *'not so great, but could be worse.'* And at least I *"had time"*.

Based on that prognosis, and the positive conversations, I was thinking that my metaphorical hourglass was top-stacked and chock full of sand.

By this time, I ALREADY had an urgency behind all my plans. I saw what happened to Aba when his hourglass broke.

I saw what happened to all of us.

The latent urgency was in place long before my own medical mayhem.

And after the diagnosis? *Please turn latent urgency to volume 11.* I was in full-on hustle mode. And I really went all-in, too.

The intention was there behind my actions sometimes, but I was mainly concerned about the value for the exchange of time.

I was really just focused on more. I always wanted more.

Meanwhile, my parents continued to inspire me. They held on even when it seemed impossible. I loved how they loved each other, and us. I loved how they inspired each other to grow, and their business sense was a part of their love.

I wanted that too. I wanted more.

So I hurried. I hustled harder. Then, I hustled even harder than that.

I worked my ass off and then worked somehow more than that for my vision of happiness for Future Alex on the other side of surgery "25 or 30 years later" down the road.

Future Alex was really going to enjoy his life.

But I still wanted more.

The power of an end in sight is unmatched as motivation.

Through sheer force of will and power of mind, I also became a media member for the UFC and the Miami Dolphins, too.

Then, I created not just one, but two 7-figure businesses all in the span of a decade.

I knew there was more to be had. I still wanted more.

Next up, I began expanding my mentorship business while helping other people scale their mentorship business to experience greater success as my entrepreneurial focus.

Things were going so well, and they were moving so fast.

But I still wanted more. I knew more was out there.

I got married to the love of my life — my highschool sweetheart — I am honestly the luckiest. We decided we wanted a family of our own. I was ecstatic because I knew that I wanted so badly to be a father, and we started planning our future.

Everything was getting better by the minute.

But I still wanted more.

And, this seems like a good time to break. **[Press pause].**

△△△

Oh, you don't think it's the right time to pause?

I didn't either.

The thing about hustling, and I know you know, is that pausing for anything that doesn't seem relevant at that very moment, no matter what it might be, is almost painful.

Okay, it actually feels painful.

Occasionally, in the middle of the hustle, I would have to have to squeeze in a dumb appointment or something that I just couldn't overwork my way out of — super irritating, right?

Stopping, pausing, and breaking for anything when I was in the middle of work was top ten, hands down, the worst thing to deal with for me.

Ever since I found out about the heart thing, it was a major inconvenience to have these regular doctor check-ups, nothing new, but I did it.

So there I was, interrupting something important to show up for an annual check-up with my normal cardiologist. And I'm in for the same old thing, right off the bat.

So, from the top:

- I enter the waiting room and join the buzz of nervous people getting their hearts checked. Never mind the fact the average age was 65+ and I'm sitting there waiting as a 28 year old.
- I get shuffled to the back and into a room — check.
- It's here I prepare for the typical sights and sounds of tests. I mentally steel myself for the cold jelly on my chest. Doesn't help — still cold and goopy, check.
- Next, the incessant beeping of the echocardiogram machine — check.
- The lights are always way too bright in here. They should do something about that — ugh, check.
- Enter the sounds of blood whooshing (much eerier than you'd think) — check, check.
- Queue the ticks of the EKG — check.
- Then, they say, all good, and see you next time — **not check.**

Wait. WHAT?!

Real talk: Between crazy fast and world-renowned runners Usain Bolt and Sir Mo Farah, who would win in a race?

To answer correctly, you need to know one more thing: the distance of the race.

The doctors just dropped the bad news bomb right in my lap.

All the hustle and overworking and non-stop crunching and long hours and anxiety and exhaustion rapidly sped up the growth of my heart.

What I thought was the solution was actually part of the problem and, in retrospect, it's all so stupidly obvious. It's actually all just *so stupid.*

I mean, what would happen to a car's engine if it was constantly in overdrive? *Yep, that's right.*

I hustled so hard and put so much stress on my heart from 18 to 28 that it sped the timeline up dramatically.

Surgery was necessary now. At 28.

I was fuming. But I could see exactly what happened.

The hustle hustled me.

The mistakes I made were crystal clear.

I understood. I knew I would have to have surgery immediately.

And I was pretty sure I couldn't hustle my way out of trouble this time.

Or could I? *Maybe a little?*

Would you believe that the very first thing I asked the doctor was, **"Can this surgery wait until March?"**

Why would I ask this?

> Listen. We were planning for our first event at the end of February. This was big.
>
> Like hell, I was going to just cancel it if there was any other way. There had to be another way.

Did you read that right?!

You did, indeed.

Even with life-altering surgery staring me in the face, the hustle had me at

> "Well, can I just get this one work thing done first?"

That's how totally brainwashed I was.

And, yes, we did run the event, and it was supremely epic, which is actually not the point, I've since learned.

The new surgery timeline was decided in December 2019, and we scheduled my aortic valve replacement for March 2020.

March 2020. Enter COVID — *ever heard of it?*

All "elective" surgeries were immediately rescheduled to forever TBD.

This news was upsetting for so many reasons. First, just COVID.

But, also, for someone whose heart was growing at a rapid pace, "elective" didn't seem like quite the right word for my surgery.

Since the growth was largely due to anxiety and stress, the delays weren't really helping my cause either.

Not to be poor, pitiful me, but how many lessons can one person even learn? *Over the line!*

△△△

Very thankfully, my wife was then, is still now, and forever will be my rock.

My family was and is strong, and this kind of thing isn't anything new for us. We'll just take care of the problem together — you know, *again*.

I tried to use this time constructively and focused on just being.

This consisted mainly of practicing "being" patient with myself because I couldn't do anything else, but also practicing not "being" in the middle of the hustle.

> Looking back, I wonder if anyone else tried to un-hustle during the pandemic? Did you?

The choice was easy for me. This time, I had to NOT hustle to survive.

My productivity entailed coming up with ways to help businesses by thinking outside the box during the pandemic.

I relied on systems and processes to investigate my own time expenditures and commitments.

I wanted to learn how differently I was spending time now versus before.

All of this I did very purposefully without sinking myself under the weight of stress.

Then, finally, they rescheduled the open heart surgery for October 2020. An end in sight!

Not the best end, admittedly, but an end nonetheless.

[An Interlude]

Before everything went haywire and I sped up my timeline with the hustle, my wife and I had been blissfully planning our future life together.

Since we learned about the looming surgery, compounded with the stress of COVID, and then with all the delays, we decided to postpone starting a family until after the surgery because, well, you know why.

Midway to the rescheduled surgery date, we found out Shira was pregnant. *Surprise!*

I'm fairly confident that more happiness and nervousness have never been crammed into one person all at once in human history.

Probably.

And so I would go into surgery when Shira was five months pregnant with our son.

[End Scene]

With all of that in mind, with everything at stake, with so much on the line, you can imagine I was experiencing some major thoughts and feels going into the hospital on surgery day.

The doctor reassured me as they were wheeling me to the OR.

Surprisingly, it was exactly what I needed to hear.

> **"Alex, don't worry. You're gonna get through this, and you're gonna be fine."**

And I'm nodding off, and I'm nodding at him at the same time. He's looking at me, and he's thumbs-upping, and then says,

> **"I promise you, you'll meet your son."**

Then, lights out.

Other than a little fundraising and some friendly trash talk, Lightning Bolt and Mobot never actually raced. Odds are, they likely won't ever.

Why not?

The answer is simple — they aren't competitors.

∆∆∆

And, lights back on.

That doctor kept his promise — at current publishing, this is not a posthumous collection.

I woke up, recovered slowly, and would go on to meet my son a few months later.

117 days after I came out of surgery, to be exact, my son was born. He's growing up healthy, happy, and the love of all of our lives.

I love being a dad more than I thought possible.

He keeps us on our toes, and he is *so fast* — **but he doesn't hustle.**

Do you know who else doesn't hustle? Usain Bolt and Mo Farah. They're fast, like, Olympic Gold medal fast, but no hustle to be found.

It's funny to think about arguably the two fastest men in the world, and *my toddler*, being able to not outrun — *but transcend* — hustle culture with a simple "no".

(Parents, you get it.)

It seemed like such a difficult decision for me to make time and time again.

But, they all seem to already know what some people take a lifetime to figure out, and when you know, you just k**no**w.

- To be successful, you have to define an end goal and have it in sight.
- Once the end goal is clear, you must design the steps and milestones it takes to get there.
- The obvious next step is the part most people skip directly to, and that's simply doing the work.
- Your end goal probably won't be the same as someone else's *(and probably shouldn't be)* so to judge your success by someone else's measure is a waste.
- If it's not the same goal, you're not competing —no matter how hard hustle culture tells you that you are.
- Your end goal can change, and it should, as your life changes.
- Goals can and should change to support happiness and an abundance of choices for the Present You and the Future you. No more allowing the Future to punish Present you..

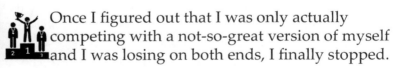

Once I figured out that I was only actually competing with a not-so-great version of myself and I was losing on both ends, I finally stopped.

A little late, I know.

I had plenty of hard knocks and life lessons along the way to help solidify my decision — a few of which I hope you don't have to experience to get it right a little sooner than I did.

The best insider info that you'll keep hearing, and not just in this handbook but also from others who have made it out, is that the secret is just to start.

You can start by just clearly defining your goals.

Once you get your footing on the ANTI-Hustle path, your journey will fall into place as you develop your purpose and intention.

But, if it can really be that simple, why aren't more people making the journey?

For the machine to continue to rumble, roll, and wreck, everyone in it has to continue to believe that success can only exist in the wake of the hustle's die-hard penchant for endless hard work.

△△△

Here's what I come up with every time:

Most hustlers, even the most hardened sharp-skilled hustling high wizards, already have at one time or currently are suppressing thoughts of doubt about some aspect of the hustle process **because hustling SUCKS.**

I said what I said.

It's painful. It's not efficient. It's not sustainable. It's harmful. It's renowned for collateral damage. The hustle is not a pleasant time, truly.

And here's one of the hustle's greatest hacks of all: If you start to even *think* hustling sucks, the hustle has rewired your brain to tell you,

> **"It's you! It's all because you're just not hustling hard enough!"**

As a result, it's totally natural for anyone, *even those seemingly successful at the hustle,* to occasionally doubt their hardline doctrine and be confused when things never seem to add up.

However, the hustle is also well-oiled and expertly maintained with *incomparable* street cred and merch, to boot.

There are so many songs and movies and ads about it, we have countless ways to subconsciously internalize hustle culture from birth to "finally sleeping when we're dead."

You'll find no shortage of self-help books, coaches, gurus, preachers, and teachers who sing the praises of the hustle gospel each and every day.

There is also an entire genre of magazines dedicated to hustling, though I'm not sure that's exactly the same kind of hustle.

I digress.

Don't forget clothes! Step right up for your "be kind & hustle hard" sweatband and a bounty of graphic prints.

Will it be a dry-fit shirt or a hat? Is the *rent always due* or *do you hustle & shine*? Those unisex muscle tees come in sizes NB-5XL and are for sale 12 months out of the year.

Don't forget flip-straw thermoses and travel coffee mugs for work! Maybe you remember those tattered half-cocked motivational materials in the old executive offices you envied so much.

"Hustle & Heart Will Set You Apart" in thin brassy frames behind each king-size desk at your first adult job.

It's very difficult to shake that much accepted "credibility," no matter how absurd it is.

In its excess, hustle culture won't ever answer for…

- How and why you don't know what "success" is
- How and why everything is so confusing
- How and why you can't touch "success" now
- How and why you're always so "busy"
- How and why you still make very little progress

Because hustle has so much (read: TOO MUCH) unchecked power, it can shuffle the blame elsewhere. It can move the goalposts whenever it likes.

And it does *all the time.*

And isn't it *just like* hustle culture to not be efficient and not be sustainable and then to wear you down, to break your spirit, and still manage to successfully convince you that YOU are the problem?

And, to solve your problem of you, what does hustle culture throw in the hat as the solution?

That's right — to get better, it looks like you just need to **hustle harder**... Maybe try 110% next time?

Have you thought about giving it your all? <— This is incredibly unhelpful.

△△△

Stay with me on this one...

Hungry?

French fries are an unassailable food. This is a fact. They're ready in no time, you can share them *(or not)*, and they're totally dippable.

Here, I want you to consider how you would react if you burned french fries in the air fryer. Easy to do, right?

Those things are a modern wonder — they heat up so quickly!

Now, imagine your partner's response to what just happened.

Did they recommend to *just burn the fries more?*

No way! *Not my wife, anyway.*

So, now what? The fries are burnt, and everyone is still hungry.

We're talking about fries, *but also not fries, okay?*

If things aren't going so well with fries, in your life, or in your business, stop and re-evaluate your approach.

Before making another choice, consider all the options you have to be successful — there are so many.

BUT, doubling down on the one thing that's definitely not working is definitely not the best option.

This is sunk cost fallacy in action.

So, I know I'm not eating the burnt fries, and neither is Shira.

And *why would we*? There is more than one way to be successful at this! We have options!

Having a process and systems in place for any — let's just say — unfortunate situation, makes things like "burning the fries" more of a non-issue.

TIP:
When you build and implement foundational processes and systems in your business and problems arise, SOPs divert crises and make mitigation manageable for you and your team. Because just experience isn't enough.

Moving forward, you can try again without everything falling apart.

AKA:
This works with way more than just burnt fries, but still also for fries.

REDO.

First thing's first. Stop to identify and re-evaluate the *actual* problem at hand.

Remember, it's not even the fries, it's the snack attack! We're all still hungry.

Now that you have regained clarity on the real problem, go back to your methods.

To solve the problem of hunger, I tried to make fries. I failed.

I made a burning heap of potato fire instead.

This is no good. I should not continue with this method of burning fries to solve the hunger problem.

Next, I need to identify other options to be successful at solving the problem: hunger.

Use your resources.

Team up. Take suggestions. Go to the drawing board of typical troubleshooting processes that you have in place.

Maybe, I first scrap the now-kindling that used to be potatoes and make a new batch or order for delivery.

Maybe I could have a PB&J. Maybe I could order a pizza.

Maybe I'll have a salad. *I should probably have a salad.* Only 1 vote for salad — veto.

Still… Options! Options! Options! Now I'm going to evaluate the potential risks and obstacles that come with my options.

With which of these choices is my success most likely?

*(Hang tough because this next part is the crux of where the trouble comes in for hustle culture enthusiasts. So, hold on to your "be kind & hustle hard" hat, **if** you're still wearing it.)*

I will make a choice that I believe will best solve my original problem with the highest likelihood of success based on the information I have combined with the experiences I've had and whatever problem-solving measures I have in place: team, processes, and systems.

But, no matter what I choose, I could still fail.

> I might accidentally burn the fries again on round two, *but maybe I won't*. Maybe the delivery order will take too long, and the fries will be cold and soggy, but *maybe it won't*.
>
> Maybe the strawberry jelly jar is in the fridge, but it's actually empty, but maybe it isn't.
>
> (Schrödinger's jelly, anyone?)

I'll continue to use the same systems and processes to try other options and weed out other solutions.

No matter what happens with the fries, I still have the foundational ideology, confidence, and resilience to take on the risk and learn from it.

Whether I end up eating choice fries that night is less important than the experience informing my options for next time to figure out the actual root issue and solve it better.

Being an ANTI-Hustler is just like that, but it isn't just with fries — it's *everything*.

When you have the foundations for success, you have more choices, and so being successful is far easier *(and much, much tastier)*.

The ANTI-Hustle Model is naturally on the other end of the spectrum to hustle culture, but they're not just opposites — they're two fundamentally different approaches.

△△△

Earlier, we talked about the dangers of measuring success by the wrong standards, whether it be limiting yourself to one narrow version of success **or** using someone else's definition of success.

Those cautionary tales are just scraping the surface of the core differences between the models. ANTI-Hustle strongly rejects the idea of pigeon-holing the definition of success to a reductive "work hard always" mantra.

Instead, you remain in charge of defining and redefining success and what it requires to achieve it by evolving standards for success for both Present You and Future You. You own it, it's yours.

YOU. ARE. IN. CHARGE.

The trick for the ANTI-Hustle to serve your needs (let's be real here — ***and your ego***) is to remain open and willing to evolve your standards as you grow and change.

The evolution of success is so essential to happiness...

Whatever you choose as a measure of success, for both now and then, must meet your needs, give you options, and never rob you of choice or time.

Present You and Future You must have equal consideration.

The ANTI-Hustle
A Continuum

△△△

As **Part I** comes to a close, think about where you are right now on your ANTI-Hustle journey as you prepare for the action steps in Part II.

ANTI-Hustle is abundance, choice, and fulfillment.

To be an ANTI-Hustler, you have access to a bounty of successes both now and in the future. Of which, you can choose how to spend your time and, by doing so, you better fulfill the promise of a successful you.

Hustle culture is founded on sacrifice, monotony, and scarcity instead.

To be a hustler, you must sacrifice anything and everything "necessary" right now for a future that has yet to be developed or determined. It might not even be a future that truly defines success for you, but just a general success for some people.

If you're still knee-deep in hustle culture, but ANTI-Hustle is where you want to go — stick around. PART II of this book is made for you.

I've been where you are and know how frustrating it is.

I also happen to know a way out.

△△△

Thanks for reading PART I of The ANTI-Hustler's Handbook

△△△

In **PART II: The ANTI-Hustle**, you'll get the exact tools and resources you need to get from where you are right now to where you want to go.

To prioritize your time, read through Chapter 1 and take the Self-Assessment.

Chapter 1 gives you the gist of how PART II is set up. Your results from the Self-Assessment will match you to the chapters that meet your specific needs right now.

From there, you can move forward with the actionable steps and tools necessary to **shift your mindset and redefine success on your ANTI-Hustle journey.**

It's so worth the trip.

— PART II —
THE ANTI-HUSTLE

ΔΔΔ

"Just over the ridge in front of you, another mountain that you'll have to climb."

— NeedToBreathe —

ΔΔΔ

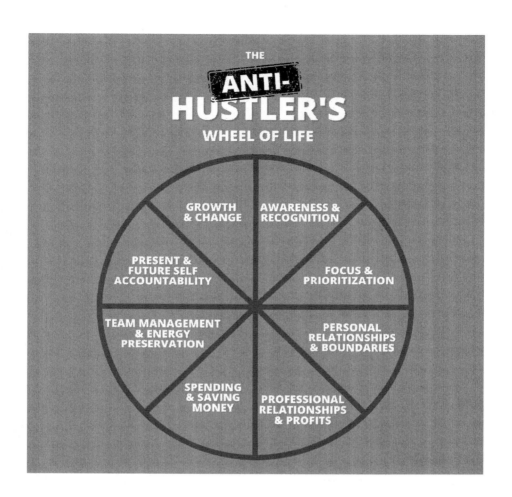

CHAPTER 01

A VICTORY LAP & SELF-ASSESSMENT

A victory lap? Already? Right at the start? Welcome to the ANTI-Hustle Model. You belong here.

The ANTI-Hustle Model posits that the goal of entrepreneurship is happiness and freedom - time & financial freedom - and choice is truly the greatest gift of running your own business.

And, just as promised at the very beginning of the book, there's *so, so much more.*

The good news for everyone, and especially those still on the hustle track, is that being ANTI-Hustle is inherently anti-busy on principle. That "so, so much more" is actually super doable.

As a result, this action-oriented section won't be chock-full of mind-bending work meant to keep you up at night or purposefully weighty material with difficult-to-understand language, entrance exam analogies, or anecdotes meant to expend all your mental calories — it's very much **not** any those things.

The upside is that The ANTI-Hustle Handbook is written for business owners.

The downside to streamlining any experience is that it can sometimes give off an 'inch deep, mile wide' vibe that makes people uncomfortable.

I don't feel uncomfortable. It's the necessary first step. Addressing weighty concepts and powerful options is exactly what you need to confidently begin your journey.

Anything more at the start would make you more uncomfortable — and potentially also make you fall asleep.

It's a wide, wild world out there that's just stuffed full of hustle culture right now. Thus, **PART II** is solely designed for accessible support for your personal growth and the growth of your business while prioritizing your time right now.

The ANTI-Hustle
PART II : A GUIDE

∧∧∧

1. The first thing to know is...

- there's <u>no wrong way</u> to read this book

2. The next thing to know is if you want more...

- background information on ideas in the second half
- insight on how PART II was put together
- behind the scenes of what's recommended here
- guidance for accessing the information in PART II

All the support you'll need for traveling through the second half of the book is available in the *Tools & Resources* sections in each chapter as well as at the end of the book.

3. Here are some options for how to journey through PART II *if you don't already have a plan in mind...*

<u>The Teeter Totter Approach</u>

- Flip around and grab *what* you need when you need it if that's what you can commit to right now.
- There's no reason to feel guilty about making even a little time to improve your life.

The Comprehensive Approach (recommended)

- Reading front to back, starting from the Introduction & Preface at the very beginning and finishing the whole book will level up your understanding and impact — *swear it*.

- The Intro & Preface build the foundation for the book, contextualize important terms, brief you on the potential and direction of the journey, and familiarize you with me.

- However, aside from being the most comprehensive, it is also the longest route.

The "I've Got 15 Minutes" Approach

- Super short on time? Heard my story before? Just interested in the action steps? **Prioritize just PART II.**

- But make sure you read Chapter 1 and take the Self-Assessment.

  The information and results there determine which chapters will match your needs to prioritize your time for the biggest impact.

- From there, you'll get specific action steps to take right now so you can start ANTI-Hustling today.

No matter how you choose to delve into PART II, the goal of every chapter is the same: *to provide you with actionable steps to beat the hustle and keep ANTI-Hustling your way to greater choices for success.*

Chapters 2-9 all have the same structure — consistency strikes again to help save your mental bandwidth.

CHAPTER OUTLINE

Title

- **FOUNDATION:** What are the basics of this ANTI-Hustle segment?
- **MINDSET:** How can the ANTI-Hustle clarify how I think about this segment?
- **ACTION:** How can you take action and start ANTI-Hustling?
- **TOOLS & RESOURCES:** What support do you need for the ANTI-Hustle journey?
- **NEXT STEPS:** How do ANTI-Hustlers reframe and reassess for success?

Outlines are helpful, but mapping your version of success and the milestones for progress will still be very difficult without identifying some kind of starting point and finish line.

My recommendation?

Read or listen to the whole book. Start at the beginning and finish it after turning over the last page.

PART I and PART II of the book are foundational and essential.

But, it's also my book — I'll try to set that aside.

△△△

PART II is what you'll wanna grab in the fire...

- In Part II, Chapter 1 and the Self Assessment are a must
- The Self Assessment results will direct you to chapters 2 - 9, depending on where you are on your ANTI-Hustle journey right now, today
- The chapters close up shop at number 10 with an overview of *The Comfort Zone* and a reminder of how to maintain your ANTI-Hustle progress
- After the chapters, the supplemental material includes the ANTI-Hustler's Toolkit with traditional backmatter.

Please pocket what works for you and employ it at will, recommend what you think will be useful to others, and, for now, leave whatever weighs you down on your journey.

The choices really are all yours.

And that's what ALL of this is for — creating more accessible choices for success. You get to choose.

△△△

There are so many options for anyone to be as successful as they want to be without sacrificing their Present Self for their Future Self.

The ANTI-Hustler's Handbook is an actionable resource for what to do when hustle culture has twisted and turned the truth so far that your own happiness becomes indistinguishable from any other well-laid plan, especially one that just happens to be borrowed from someone else.

The hustle is renowned for making the truth so unrecognizable that you'll believe just about anything is "necessary" for your future success, even if you stopped recognizing yourself in that future.

Rather than continue to play a version of yourself in your own life, you can tap into the abundance of choices that the ANTI-Hustle journey provides.

You have access to...

- my story to make connections between your experiences and someone else's. The hustle feels like a lonely road, but that's just part of the trick. It actually sucks for everyone — you're not alone.

- expanded online tools and resources that will benefit Present You right now to get out of the constant race for Future You.

- an abundance of resources in this book that Present You needs now to start getting your footing on your ANTI-Hustle journey. The truth is, *there isn't only one way to be successful* when you add more choices for success to your life.

Of these, perhaps, the first and most important choice in your new arsenal of options might be: to leave the endless hustle marathon *once and for all.*

You have the power to choose.

I did, and the ANTI-Hustle changed my life.

I have more to be thankful for RIGHT NOW than I ever dreamed possible AND Future Me is already set up for a slow clap too.

I want that for you and everyone – **one big victory lap.**

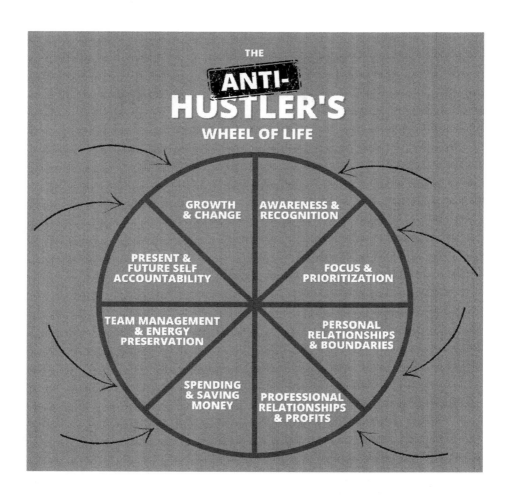

THE ANTI-HUSTLE
SELF-ASSESSMENT

Hustle: Strives for faster and more.
Values the pursuit of success and hyper-productivity.

ANTI-Hustle: Strives for sustainability and balance.
Values evolution of choices and success.

FOUNDATION

"When the pain of staying the same is greater than the pain of change you must change"

∆∆∆

One of my personal mentors, William Attaway, finds a way to apply the perfect quote to any frame of mind a person could be in at any given time. It's a gift, really. He always finds just the one — be it for wins, losses, progress… and even the pain of change.

ABOUT THE ANTI-HUSTLE SELF ASSESSMENT
On Purpose

- The purpose of the self-assessment is for you to learn how best to balance your life now, for your Present Self to enjoy the opportunities you have while setting your Future Self up for more choices that will increase your happiness, otherwise known as *true success.*

- The self-assessment is a quick and easy evaluation using the *ANTI-Hustler's Wheel of Life* to determine the impact of hustle culture on you right now.

On Starting Points

The numbering for BOTH starts at 2, not 1. Don't freak out, this isn't a mistake.

- ANTI-Hustle Wheel of Life starts at #2
- The matching segment chapters start at #2

On High/Low Scores

- The goal here *isn't* your typical high score - (don't fall prey to 36%)
- The goal *is* to honestly identify which areas in your life are more balanced and which need the most support

On Assessments

- No matter the explanation or the pretense, latent anxiety and resistance typically exist with test-taking
- Don't let that deter you. Grab a seat, settle in with your beverage of choice, and really think it through
- Both Present You and Future You will be glad you did

On Scoring Guidance

Your score for each wheel segment will be a '1' or a '0'

- 1 = yes - I do say or often hear that
- 0 = no - I do not say or never hear that

On Scoring Clarity

What does it mean... *"I do say or often hear that"?* When you read each segment, evaluate each hustle-ism there, and ask yourself two questions about each one:

Q: Do I ever say these things? and/or
Q: Do I ever hear these things?

For "yes," meaning you either have heard or said the hustle-ism statement, enter a '1' in the corresponding score box.

For "no," meaning you neither have heard nor said the hustle-ism statement, enter a '0' in the corresponding score box.

On Example Practice

In the following example segment, I scored 3 out of 5.

This means I, myself, (yes) either had heard or said "Hustle and heart will set you apart," "No rest for the wicked," and "There's no 'overtime' in owning your own business - it's called 'all-the-time'."

This also means that I (no) neither heard nor said, "I'll sleep when I'm dead." or "Me and The Rock have the same 24 hours in a day."

After tallying my marks, I wrote the total score for this segment at the bottom, which is how I know I got 3 out of 5 for this segment/chapter.

EXAMPLE SEGMENT

Remember, for each one, you're asking yourself:
Have I said or heard this?

- If "**yes**," mark a "1" in the box.
- If "**no**," mark a "0" in the box.

	AWARENESS & RECOGNITION	
	Have I said or heard this before?	YES = 1
1.	"Why am I so stressed *all the time?*"	1
2.	"Love?! I don't even know if I LIKE what I'm doing anymore."	0
3.	"Do I even want this anymore? Is it worth all the sacrifice?"	1
4.	"Is it really supposed to be this hard?"	1
5.	"I'm at my breaking point, I'm burned out."	0
TOTAL SCORE OUT OF 5		**3 / 5**

Just like I said, I marked my 3 / 5 at the bottom. I'll continue on to the next section and do the same until each segment is complete — easy enough.

Before you do the real thing, a disclaimer:

Making a major shift in your life is a big deal - you're doing tough work.

The coming assessment and subsequent chapters are meant to provide clarity, but that can also be uncomfortable if the pain of staying the same becomes too great.

If you ever feel overwhelmed with what you're learning or implementing on your ANTI-Hustle journey, it is okay to take a break.

Honoring your progress can also be achieved by reflecting on how far you have come.

There are plenty of tools and tactics both here and in the online resources that are available to support you on the next leg of your journey when you're ready to continue.

HOW TO TAKE THE SELF ASSESSMENT

1. Read the Hustle-isms listed for each segment
2. Add one point for each Hustle-ism that you have said or that you have heard
3. Add up all the points for that segment
4. Record the total out of _/5 points
5. Repeat the process until all the segments have been assessed and scored
6. Whichever segment has the highest score, turn to that corresponding chapter to begin your ANTI-Hustle journey

Take The ANTI-Hustle
SELF-ASSESSMENT

△△△

AWARENESS & RECOGNITION

	Have I said or heard this before?	YES = 1
1.	"Why am I so stressed *all the time*?"	
2.	"Love?! I don't even know if I LIKE what I'm doing anymore."	
3.	"Do I even want this anymore? Is it worth all the sacrifice?"	
4.	"Is it really supposed to be this hard?"	
5.	"I'm at my breaking point, I'm burnt out."	
TOTAL SCORE OUT OF 5		___ / 5

If your score is high in this section, Chapter 2 has the ANTI-Hustle Solutions.

FOCUS & PRIORITIZATION

	Have I said or heard this before?	YES = 1
1.	Even though you don't have time... "Sure, I have time", "Yeah, I can make that happen", "No, it's not a bad time", "I can take that on"	
2.	"I'm running a little late from a few things that got pushed back this morning, can we push our call 15-30 minutes?"	
3.	"There's so much on my plate right now that I have no idea what to do first."	
4.	"My calendar is stacked, I'll have to push this to next week."	
5.	"If you could just give me one second before we get started, I just need to take care of a few things really quickly."	
TOTAL SCORE OUT OF 5		___ / 5

If your score is high in this section, Chapter 3 has the ANTI-Hustle Solutions.

PERSONAL RELATIONSHIPS & BOUNDARIES

	Have I said or heard this before?	YES = 1
1.	"I know it's important to you and I said that I would, but I just can't __. I'll make it happen next time though."	
2.	"I spend more time at work than I do at home."	
3.	"This is my work wife/husband."	
4.	"Listen, what's your problem? You know how much pressure I'm under with this big deadline."	
5.	"I'm sorry it took so long to get back to you."	
TOTAL SCORE OUT OF 5		___ / 5

If your score is high in this section, Chapter 4 has the ANTI-Hustle Solutions.

PROFESSIONAL RELATIONSHIPS & PROFITS

	Have I said or heard this before?	YES = 1
1.	"I'm just trying to squeeze as much money as I can out of him/her."	
2.	"I'm struggling to manage all these opportunities. There's just too much to do."	
3.	"I've been working on this big deal for months! Is this thing ever going to actually close?!?"	
4.	"[Competitor] just got lucky, they didn't even have to work for it."	
5.	"I hate dealing with [client], but I need the money."	
TOTAL SCORE OUT OF 5		___ / 5

If your score is high in this section, Chapter 5 has the ANTI-Hustle Solutions.

SPENDING & SAVING MONEY

Have I said or heard this before?	YES = 1
1. "No way I have enough money yet — even the average millionaire has AT LEAST 7 streams of income."	
2. "Everyone knows you have to pay to play, invest to impress, or let your money talk when you enter a room."	
3. "I'm not exactly sure what my profit is month-over-month. I know it's something I should be more on top of."	
4. "[Competitor] is already at 6 figures a month. Where are MY 6-figure months?! Let's pivot to what they're doing."	
5. "Cutting staff and salaries are where the real savings are — especially with all this AI, how could you NOT."	
TOTAL SCORE OUT OF 5	___ / 5

If your score is high in this section, Chapter 6 has the ANTI-Hustle Solutions.

TEAM MANAGEMENT & ENERGY PRESERVATION

Have I said or heard this before?	YES = 1
1. "My team is not pulling their weight. I'm doing too much!"	
2. "I can do this faster myself."	
3. "Only I can do [insert task] correctly."	
4. "Hiring someone will take too long."	
5. "If I automate, the tech will break or something will get lost in the mix — I just know it."	
TOTAL SCORE OUT OF 5	___ / 5

If your score is high in this section, Chapter 7 has the ANTI-Hustle Solutions.

PRESENT & FUTURE SELF ACCOUNTABILITY

	Have I said or heard this before?	YES = 1
1.	"My actual life right now and where I thought I'd be at this point in my life are very, very different."	
2.	"Life isn't the greatest at this exact moment, but that's all going to change when ___ happens."	
3.	"What?! No. My dream life is nothing like my life right now."	
4.	"You have to hustle to win — you're playing a dangerous game by telling people this BS."	
5.	"Pretend all you want, but it IS a competition — EVERYTHING is — there will always be judges, winners, and losers."	
TOTAL SCORE OUT OF 5		___ / 5

If your score is high in this section, Chapter 8 has the ANTI-Hustle Solutions.

GROWTH & CHANGE

	Have I said or heard this before?	YES = 1
1.	"Look, it's just not going to happen. I tried the best I could, and it is what it is."	
2.	"Ugh! I shouldn't have listened to anyone else — this happens every single time."	
3.	"I'm on the hot mess express, struggle-bussin' my way to the end of the day."	
4.	"Failure isn't an option. I'll figure it out on my own — I have to. I put a lot of money and time into this."	
5.	"I should already be there by now."	
TOTAL SCORE OUT OF 5		___ / 5

If your score is high in this section, Chapter 9 has the ANTI-Hustle Solutions.

△△△

Congratulations!

You just ANTI-Hustled your way through the Self-Assessment!

△△△

Next Steps

1. Compare Scores:
Next, compare the scores in each section to find out where to seek out ANTI-Hustle support and where you already have more balance.

2. Evaluate Impact:
To evaluate the current impact of hustle culture on each area of your life, refer to…

THE SEGMENT SCORING GUIDE

- 0-1 Points =
  You're ANTI-hustling it here.

- 2-3 Points =
  You've been hit by the hustle here.

- 4-5 Points =
  You're most hurt by the hustle here.

3. Match Chapters and Needs

- For the best use of your time and energy, you need to prioritize the chapters that will help you the most on your specific ANTI-Hustle journey right now.
- Return to your segment scores.
- Next, identify the segment with the highest score and mark that chapter as #1 on your list of priorities.
- Turn to your #1 priority chapter to begin your ANTI-Hustle journey right now
- When finished, you will move to the chapter with the next highest score, and then the next highest, and so on...

4. What happens if there's a tie?

- It happens. *It's just that way sometimes.*
- If there's a tie, celebrate having more than one option for success! *You're doing it!*
- Choose to prioritize the chapter that makes the most sense to you for your life *right now*.

5. Next, be sure to calculate the Total Balance Factor.

- Once you've finished evaluating each segment to determine its priority, add up all the totals.
- All of the totals added together comprise your TBF or *Total Balance Factor*.
- Since there are 8 total segments, there are 40 possible Balance Points.
- Record the Total Balance Factor as (TBF# /40)

6. Use the ANTI-Hustler Progress Report below to record data each time you take the Self-Assessment

Record: the date, the segment totals, and Total Balance Factor (TBF) # /40

The purpose of the **ANTI-Hustler Progress Report** is to track the ways in which you maintain balance in certain areas of your life or how your balance might otherwise ebb and flow within the different seasons of your life.

As you define what success looks like for you and open up more choices, a better understanding of how you typically balance certain areas of your life is ideal.

THE ANTI-HUSTLE PROGRESS REPORT
BALANCING SUCCESS IN THE ANTI-HUSTLER'S WHEEL OF LIFE

DATE	SLICE 1	SLICE 2	SLICE 3	SLICE 4	SLICE 5	SLICE 6	SLICE 7	SLICE 8	TBF#/40
1/3/22	3	2	1	4	3	5	1	5	24/40

NOTES

AVERAGE YOUR SCORES OVER TIME

- **33-40 Points =**
  Hustle Culture has deeply affected the balance in your life for as long as you can remember

- **25-32 Points =**
  Hustle Culture has significantly affected the balance in your life for some time

- **17-24 Points =**
  The balance in your life is regularly impacted by The Hustle, but you want something to change

- **9-16 Points =**
  The balance in your life topples occasionally, but you're ready for the next ANTI-Hustle level

- **0-8 Points =**
  The balance in your life stays close to equilibrium, but you also want to ensure it stays that way

NOTES

TIME TO START PRIORITIZING!

You just ANTI-Hustled your way through Chapter 1!

CHAPTER RESOURCES

Access ALL the resources in this chapter and more at:
https://antihustlehandbook.com/toolbox

REMEMBER

As you progress, come back to the Self Assessment, again and again, to reassess your priorities on the ANTI-Hustle journey

Each time, record the date, individual segment scores, and the Total Balance Factor to map your growth

ONWARD

1. For now, go check your scores on the Self-Assessment

2. Identify which segment/chapter is your top priority now

3. Head there and dig in where it matters most, ANTI-Hustler

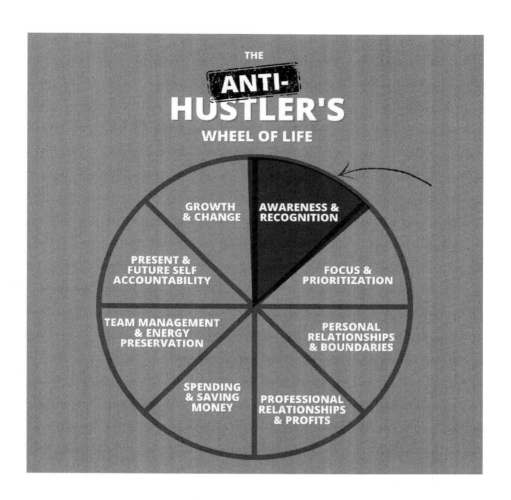

CHAPTER 02

AWARENESS & RECOGNITION

FOUNDATION

△△△

Start by thinking back to what brought you here.

All the static makes it impossible to hear the signal trying to find clarity through **Awareness & Recognition.**

Here's a quick review of what's making it so hard to hear the sweet sounds of success...

AWARENESS & RECOGNITION

- *"Why am I so stressed all the time?"*
- *"Love?! I don't even know if I LIKE what I'm doing anymore"*
- *"Do I even want this anymore? Is this worth all the sacrifice?"*
- *"Is it really supposed to be this hard?"*
- *"I'm at my breaking point — I'm burnt out"*

△△△

Bad news and good news, right?

Bad news: you're drowning.

Good news: at least you know it.

A friend once told me the key to genuine happiness is "the overcoming of known obstacles."

Then why is it so freakin' easy to get caught up in the thick of it? And it's so easy to then feel like you belong there like you've always been there. What is *THAT*?

The hustle is rife with opportunities to get wrapped up and carried away, but awareness and recognition are the skeleton keys to unlocking the emergency exit.

To be aware is to acknowledge that there is a problem — maybe it's just that you know something isn't quite right.

Something's off. But what is it? *What is it?* Ah-ha. You think, maybe it's work. It's too much right now. It doesn't feel sustainable anymore. Can you keep doing this? For how long?

You know you're juggling too much. You know you're not operating how you should be because of it. Nothing really seems that different, but this just keeps happening. The feeling. The overload. The overwhelm.

Except, now it's getting worse. Now you're really digging deep to try to figure this out.

Is it you? Is there actually more work? Is your team letting you down? Is it the clients? Are people different? I mean, AITA? Surely, SITA?!

And the worst part of all this? *I know you already know.* You honestly believe right now that if you just work a little harder, for just a little longer, you'll get out from under this whole thing.

You believe that there has to be a light at the end of this hustle tunnel. There has to be, right? This can't go on forever.

This is just temporary – some kind of Post-COVID influx of weird business flow that hasn't leveled out. That's all it is.

But is it though? Is that all this is?

MINDSET

∧∧∧

Freeing up your head space will help calm and focus your attention on the task at hand.

The Brain Dump lets you know that work is here and now, for now.

That said, it's time.

The ANTI-Hustle BRAIN DUMP

1. Grab your handy dandy ANTI-Hustler's Companion Handbook at https://antihustlehandbook.com/toolbox
2. Flip to the Brain Dump Prompt for Chapter 2: **Where is my overwhelm stemming from right now?**
3. Put 10 minutes on the clock, and start writing!
4. Do the thing and once the timer dings, continue reading below with newfound clarity.

Hey, look at you — more clarity by the minute.

Ironically, the same awareness and clarity that helps solve overwhelm is also the root cause of serious anxiety and depression for many still trapped in the hustle.

The pressure of massive overwhelm often causes claustrophobic fears of being closed in by inadequacy. The results can be paralyzing, and the negative impacts are long-lasting.

The self-limiting beliefs at one point make it simply impossible to conceive of ever being able to consistently claw out of the crushing overwhelm. But, you can and you will. I know because I was there.

They say you can drown in an inch of water, but that's not what this is. For many entrepreneurs, the overwhelm is so great, they struggle to keep their head above 'do not swim — strong current' water with waves crashing down overhead.

So, how'd you get in over your head anyway?

For me, those Hustle-isms point to a few common underlying issues. It's definitely no secret that entrepreneurs can have a lot of different issues — *big laugh, right?* It doesn't feel very funny as it's happening, I know that much.

When I hear certain concerns, I know they're just symptomatic of bigger underlying challenges that a business owner is facing.

With awareness and recognition, the overwhelm is what really starts to cause major unrest, but where does it stem from?

Limited Resources

Money isn't the most important thing, but it feels like the most important thing until you have it in order.

Limited financial resources hinder the ability to invest in marketing, promotional activities, and many other aspects necessary for reinvesting in your business — let alone your personal life.

Sometimes the lack of funding is what entrepreneurs point to for lack of clarity because they can't hire teams, collect good data, or buy the best parts, and and and…

Everyone knows that no one wins the blame game.

Competition

I don't have to say this or write it because no one needs to start sweating. Things are highly competitive out there in Hustle Culture — that's how it's designed.

The stage is small, and there is not much room to share the spotlight.

Many clients complain that they have to keep working harder and harder to stand out and gain recognition. Standing out from competitors in a genuine way is crucial for gaining awareness, but they lack clarity on how.

Choice Paralysis

Ever been faced with numerous options related to your business only to walk away having not chosen anything? Left major clients or decisions on the drawing board for the weekend to think it over or sleep on it? What may sound like "careful decision-making" can sometimes devolve into bad habits like procrastination that lead to suboptimal choices.

Lack of Network

Entrepreneurs who are just starting out may not have an extensive network of connections in their industry, limiting their opportunities for exposure, collaboration, and support. The most important thing here is support.

This is not the time to eschew the advice of someone who has accomplished a life you admire.

If you have clarity on your version of success, find others that can mirror your happiness. Building relationships with key stakeholders, such as customers, suppliers, and industry influencers, is vital for increasing awareness of achieving it.

Lack of Clarity

Entrepreneurs struggle MIGHTILY with a lack of clarity regarding anything from client acquisition, how to onboard, productivity strategies, HR policies, and procedures, protecting sanity, setting boundaries, defining and setting goals and the necessary steps to achieve them, lunch, anything…

The hustle mantra of "if I just work harder, it'll come to me" is what is leading to the major impending danger and little dark cloud feelings of overwhelm — constantly.

As a result, you've clipped your own wings when trying to effectively plan and execute strategies to ultimately grow and scale.

The next step is to free yourself from this cycle.

ACTION

△△△

Now it's time to take action and quiet the Hustle-isms.

Which tool will help you quiet the Hustle-isms for *Awareness & Recognition* and gain more clarity on the common obstacles in this chapter for entrepreneurs?

The ANTI-Hustle HAPPINESS QUOTIENT

Have you ever considered there might be an actual formula for success?

Hustle Culture's "success" formula looks something like this:

Consistent Hard Work + Sacrifice = Financial Freedom

That's not the end all be all of their success formulae, but it's at least a starting point we can all agree on.

The great thing about being an entrepreneur is exercising agency and the ability to choose.

So rather than someone else defining your "success formula", you have the capability to change the arithmetic at any time.

May I be so bold as to offer a conjecture?

Your success level correlates to your happiness level.

Hear me out.

Scientists, Doctors, Entrepreneurs, Bio-Hackers, and everyone in between have all been researching happiness for decades.

Tests, tools, dissertations, and research papers are all dedicated to the topic.

My personal favorite has always been The Happiness Quotient **(HQ)**. The Happiness Quotient offers a legit formula for success:

$$\frac{\text{7 ELEMENTS}}{\text{HAPPINESS}} = \text{SUCCESS}$$

The HQ is an assessment for people to objectively judge and measure their own happiness in 7 key categories of their life.

If you're thinking...

> "But Alex, happiness doesn't pay the bills"

Yes, I know — the HQ by itself will not magically make your business more profitable.

Will anything? Not magically, no.

The more abundance in your life, the more effective you'll be at scaling your business though, and, the happier you are, the more you work in abundance and with fulfillment.

So if we agree that we all want to be happy, then we can agree this is a vital exercise for ANTI-Hustlers to break free from the grips of Hustle Culture.

The point of the HQ is to create awareness.

You can't just go in blazing without an initial understanding of your baseline happiness no matter how happy your intentions are.

Hustle Culture has a different ideology:

- No matter what the problem is, the answer is to "work harder" to solve any and all of your problems.
- Also you are probably the problem.
- Also you are not hustling hard enough.

This is no good. This doesn't work.

Without generating at least a little awareness and trying to determine what the actual problem is (it's not just you) then nothing will ever change.

Without creating a baseline, you'll never know where to start and how to map out your journey to mark your progress.

How will you know if you are hitting your marks? *(it's not because you aren't hustling hard enough).* Without tracking your progress and reassessing your plan, there's never a finish line. There is never achieved success.

There has to be a finish line. You deserve to be successful AND happy. The HQ is a life wheel that breaks down your happiness into 7 core elements.

The 7 Elements of The Happiness Quotient

1. Vision
2. Fitness
3. Family
4. Friends
5. Finances
6. Career
7. Fulfillment

Borrow My Notes

- The HQ is not a scientific test of happiness
- There are no right or wrong answers
- Every person will weigh the importance of each of the 7 elements differently
- Some people may change out one of the core 7 elements altogether

Q: Isn't the ANTI-Hustler Wheel of Life already a big part of this book? Why am I recommending yet another "wheel of life" type exercise?

A: One solution isn't for everyone — *ever heard of it?*

About the Assessment

Carve out approximately 15 minutes to complete the whole thing, maybe a little less. Afterward, there are also two journal sections that offer further insight.

> *My favorite version of the HQ was inspired by thehappinesshunter.com but don't worry because you can still find the ANTI-Hustler version at https://antihustlehandbook.com/toolbox — options.*

After completing the assessment...

First, count it as essential to reflect on the entire experience. Gaining perspective through evaluation is a crucial step in "what's next?"

Action planning power...

That second journal opportunity is also your shot at a really manageable action plan. You'll choose 3 actions to prioritize within a set deadline in order to improve your HQ scores.

Movement. Progress. Purpose.

You're set up to make some really good choices right now.

Choices are a good thing, and the HQ is set up to be empowering, not debilitating.

Aside from a strengthened foundation for making choices for your own happiness, you also gained something else out of this — more clarity.

Mama didn't raise any fool - you *already* know something isn't right. So you were already aware there was a problem: in that case, you have one or more areas of your life where you're already dissatisfied.

What IS NEW is your ability to choose to take action.

With clarity on where you lack happiness, you have identified and can now choose to optimize — that you know how to do.

You are moving in the right direction toward your definition of success.

Look at you go ANTI-Hustler... Look. At. You. Go.

TOOLS & RESOURCES

△△△

Access ALL the resources in this chapter and more at:
https://antihustlehandbook.com/toolbox

1. **Treasure Map:**
   Consider this as your personal "Yellow Brick Road." What's the goal we're working towards, and the activities and milestones needed to achieve it?

2. **Overwhelm Assessment:**
   Overwhelm is the outcome of a lack of clarity. Use the assessment to forge your path ahead

3. **Mountains You've Climbed:**
   An inspiring journal prompt to help you realize how far you've come

THE CLOSER:
THE REFRAMING TECHNIQUE

△△△

Before you go, really reflect on the progress you've made over the course of just this chapter. Revisit the Hustle-isms from the start of Awareness & Recognition.

Right now is the perfect time to silence the noise and strengthen the signal.

Reframe the -isms that got you stuck to begin with.

Trade them out for empowering statements that will help you shift your mindset and strengthen your commitment to a more balanced and intentional life.

	AWARENESS & RECOGNITION: REFRAME	
	From Hustle-ism... *Why am I so stressed all the time?*	**To ANTI-Hustle-ism...** *I'm in my flow state, my comfort zone*
1.	"Why am I so stressed *all the time?*"	
2.	"Love?! I don't even know if I LIKE what I'm doing anymore."	
3.	"Do I even want this anymore? Is it worth all the sacrifice?"	
4.	"Is it really supposed to be this hard?"	
5.	"I'm at my breaking point, I'm burnt out."	

NEXT STEPS

You just ANTI-Hustled your way through Chapter 2!

∆∆∆

REMEMBER

Return to the **Self Assessment**, again and again, to reassess your growth on the ANTI-Hustle journey

Each time, record the date, individual segment scores, and the **Total Balance Factor** to map your progress

ONWARD

1. Go back and check your scores on **Self-Assessment**

2. Identify which segment & chapter you prioritized up next

3. Head there and dig in where it matters most, ANTI-Hustler

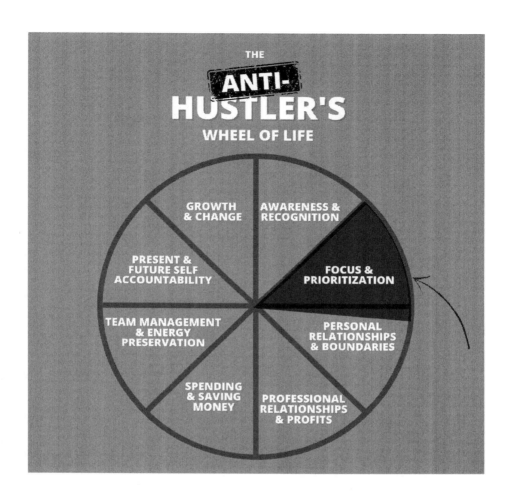

— CHAPTER 03 —
FOCUS & PRIORITIZATION

FOUNDATION

△△△

Right now, struggling to find clarity through focus and prioritization might seem like a daunting task, but it's not impossible.

Let's start with a quick review of the Focus & Prioritization Hustle-isms from the Self-Assessment that make it hard for you to hear the sweet sounds of success.

FOCUS & PRIORITIZATION

- *Even though you don't have time... "Sure, I have time", "Yeah, I can make that happen", "No, it's not a bad time", "I can take that on"*
- *"I'm running a little late from a few things that got pushed back this morning, can we push our call 15-30 minutes?"*
- *"There's so much on my plate right now that I have no idea what to do first."*
- *"My calendar is stacked, I'll have to push this to next week."*
- *"If you could just give me one second before we get started, I just need to take care of a few things really quickly."*

Ever been just totally wide awake at 2 AM thinking about a client?

Do you get your steps in while the rest of the world somehow manages to sleep because you can't stop thinking about your business?

So, how bad is it?

Are you at the "I actually only need about 3-4 hours of sleep a night to be productive the next day" phase?

Any chance you're completely and totally overwhelmed with the number of tasks you're responsible for on a regular basis?

Or have you actually managed to "optimize" your circadian rhythm on top of everything else? Keep me posted on that.

When things start to get loose at the seams, it's a good idea to step back and take a good look to see where you need to tighten things up, where you need help tightening things up, and where you might not be able to add another notch at all right now. You're up all night and dragging through the day scrambling instead of stepping back.

But, why? *Right, the hustle.*

Here's the thing — I know you truly believe that hard work and that one "big push" is all you need to get this one last thing over with and then things will be different. And, I would be totally remiss if I didn't mention that more than a few things certainly have been pushed over the finish line by the hustle.

I also would be remiss if I didn't mention that hustle power might not be as effective as you imagined because it seems like you've been pushing for a while now.

Just push through...

Just work harder, faster, and *more* so you can push past this overwhelming feeling of impending failure. Things are *this close* to turning around.

Just push through...

Get over that "last big hump" by just doing it yourself, you don't have time to deal with going back and forth with other people right now. The weight of the metric ton on your chest is so close to lifting.

Just push through…

Wake up earlier, work later, multitask, and overschedule so you don't miss any opportunities "to improve." Reach ultimate efficiency, leaving no downtime. For a little while the lists will get longer and the days shorter, but it will pay off.

I know you believe if you can just push through…

> Once this hard work is done, surely there's respite. No more work all the time. No more thinking about business all the time. Success is on the way. It has to be.

To get there faster, you'll hustle harder and give more than you have. But time passes you by again and again without change.

Working so hard was only supposed to be a final push – it was never supposed to be sustainable because it's not.

The Hustle-isms become self-talk: Push the rock up back the hill again and stop complaining.

You're no longer "pushing through" anything. The way you're working isn't a season any more than you're actually progressing toward your goals.

The only things you're progressing toward are frustration and burnout. No good foundation is made of 1-ton bricks.

MINDSET

△△△

Freeing up your head space will help calm and focus your attention on the task at hand.

The Brain Dump lets you know that work is here and now, for now.

That said, *it's time.*

The ANTI-Hustle BRAIN DUMP

1. Grab your handy dandy ANTI-Hustler's Companion Handbook at https://antihustlehandbook.com/toolbox

2. Flip to the Brain Dump Prompt for Chapter 3: **How are you currently organizing your to-do list?**

3. Put 10 minutes on the clock, and start writing!

4. Do the thing and once the timer dings, continue reading below with newfound clarity.

Hey, *look at you* — more clarity by the minute.

∆∆∆

Google translate, please…

- **Distraction:** Staying focused on long-term goals instead of getting distracted by short-term activities is one of the most important components of success.

- **Chaos:** Instead of haphazardly tackling tasks as they come, you can rely on routine procedures that help keep you organized and efficient. You can free up more time for focusing on other areas of your life or business.

- **Overwhelm:** With such an abundance of tasks, projects, and commitments, it can be hard to know where to begin or which ones deserve your attention.

- **Full-plating:** You don't need to do it all. Outsourcing can help take tedious and time-consuming tasks off your plate, freeing up more time to focus on what you do best.

- **Procrastination:** When faced with large and intimidating tasks, frustration is a natural response. However, delaying the decision-making and holding off on taking action only creates further stress.

So how do you ANTI-Hustle your way to progress?

The most straightforward strategies will help overcome decision paralysis, prioritize tasks, and delegate effectively.

ACTION

△△△

Now it's time to take action and quiet the Hustle-isms, but beware: the ANTI-Hustle journey is constantly bombarded with distractions.

Now more than ever, it is so important for entrepreneurs to maintain a sense of purposeful focus.

To do so, entrepreneurs must:

- Make appropriate goals and plans
- Stay focused on those goals
- Remain aware of potential distractions

Straightforward enough.

With increased awareness of potential threats to your progress, you can make informed decisions that are impactful.

Knowing where threats persist, for example, is critical in the allocation of resources.

Next, by keeping attention squarely on your top goals, you can better stay motivated and avoid getting sidetracked.

So, Alex, which goals are the top goals? Is that the most important or the ones at the top of the stack or the most recent or...

Don't feel bad! Don't be embarrassed. Knowing there's a problem is the first step to solving it.

This is a VERY real question that gets asked all the time.

The truth is, knowing which items to prioritize is a honed skill.

As an entrepreneur, you are constantly bombarded with a never-ending to-do list of tasks **that all seem urgent.**

I say it all the time,

- *If everything is urgent, then nothing is urgent.*
- *If everything is important, then nothing is important.*

It is difficult to decide which tasks to tackle first and which can wait. But this is exactly the time to use systems and processes for prioritization. This is when they don't just 'come in handy', but your quality of life diminishes without them.

Goal: Avoid spending time on unimportant tasks.

How to do it: Figure out which tasks are the most important.

You can choose exactly what you want to focus on, what needs to be delegated, or what can be eliminated from your task list altogether.

The tool of choice for *Focus & Prioritization?*

The ANTI-Hustle Eisenhower Matrix

PDDE, President Dwight D. Eisenhower himself, said it best:

> *"What is important is seldom urgent and what is urgent is seldom important."*

Remember, even if it was somehow possible to do everything you need to do all at once — it's certainly not smart.

Despite dreaming and the best drawing board plans, it's still highly unlikely to wake up one day with inbox zero for your to-dos.

Just from a purely entrepreneurial standpoint, everything else aside, when is everything done-done?

Even if it was, part of the definition of an entrepreneur includes: (n.) human who has a seemingly never-ending fascination with a very particular and peculiar kind of tinkering called optimization — *that's op-teh-my-zay-shun.*

Prioritizing your to-dos and tasks *(and tinkering)* with the Eisenhower Matrix is your key to freedom.

How To Begin

1. Start by brain-dumping every personal and professional task you have in your mind.

2. Separate the tasks into 2 buckets: Personal & Professional

3. Use the 4 D's of the **Eisenhower Matrix** to organize your task lists in the 4 quadrants (do a separate matrix on personal & professional tasks and do not do them together)

4. The matrix never lies about your best course of action. Trust it.

5. Utilize this tool daily, weekly, monthly, or whenever you see fit. Just know it's never wrong to ensure you're prioritizing the right tasks.

But the question remains: **How do you figure out the level of urgency and importance of a task?**

Say less…

Here's an option for figuring out the level of urgency and the importance of a task — keep reading for a quick definition of Urgent & Important to use as a guide when prioritizing your To-Do list.

- **URGENT:** A task that requires immediate attention to complete

- **IMPORTANT:** A task that is vital to your long-term goals or mission

With those two important terms defined let's urgently break down each of the four quadrants.

Starting from the top left quadrant and moving clockwise from there…

Important & Urgent

This is where the majority of hustlers work, and it's a problem because not everything in here is important and urgent at all times — that's too much, and it's a bit of a cry wolf.

For any task put into this quadrant, perhaps take the time to reconsider your position on the matter or, at the very least, investigate it fully.

- Why is this so important to me?
- Why does this need to be completed now?

If a task is truly categorized in this quadrant, that means it will contribute to your long-term goals, vision, and mission, and it also can not be pushed off to any later time.

The word associated with this quadrant is often "Do", so be wary of this quadrant as you will likely be spending a large majority of your time here.

Remember, life becomes much less stressful when you recognize the majority of your urgent tasks were never that urgent in the first place.

Important & Not Urgent

The Important & Not Urgent tasks are often the most essential, especially for ANTI-Hustlers…

- have a compounding effect on your long-term goals, vision, and mission for your life and business.
- require deep work that must be meticulously planned in order to have the biggest impact.
- this quadrant often has the term "Schedule" alongside it — that's because you'll need to carve out time for these tasks.

Scheduling time for non-urgent, but very important work, is a key indicator of successful ANTI-Hustlers.

Don't keep kicking the can down the road on these important tasks. They matter and are important for a reason.

Schedule the time and really prioritize here.

Urgent & Not Important

ANTI-Hustlers understand the value of delegation. They know it's impossible to achieve everything they want in their life and business, juggling every personal and professional responsibility by themselves.

You need help. We all need help. That is not a weakness. Having a support system is a strength. Be strong enough to recognize tasks that need immediate attention but aren't important enough for your time.

In this quadrant, we're talking about tasks that completely drain your energy without moving you one step closer to your goals.

Tasks like…

- handling a disgruntled client email
- posting on social media
- sending a weekly email to your list
- responding to an unexpected text
- a review request from a vendor

Exhausted thinking about it? Me too.

Time is such a limited resource, and it's non-renewable. Learn to identify what someone else can handle for you, so you can stay focused on the more important things in your life.

Not Urgent & Not Important

This quadrant is the real magic of the Eisenhower Matrix. It gives us permission to say "No" to tasks that don't benefit us.

When we don't prioritize our tasks, we have a binary view of everything on our to-do list.

That leads us to waste precious time on tasks that are not urgent and not important.

These mindless to-dos drain your energy, destroy productivity, and stagnate your growth.

Worse off, these tasks trick you into thinking you've "accomplished so much" off your to-do list, only to realize you still have so much left to do…

You'll see the word "Delete" associated with these tasks, and that's self-explanatory, right?

TOOLS & RESOURCES

△△△

Access ALL the resources in this chapter and more at:
https://antihustlehandbook.com/toolbox

1. **Daily Focus:**
   A productivity tool that not only teaches you how to prioritize your tasks daily but also shows you how to batch your tasks appropriately

2. **Productivity Strategies:**
   A Google Doc with 10 strategies, written by the productivity queen herself, my wife Shira

3. **5 Questions To Clarity:**
   A Google Sheet with 5 prompts to help you identify what tasks can be automated, delegated, or outright dumped altogether

THE CLOSER
THE REFRAMING TECHNIQUE

△△△

Before you go, really reflect on the progress you've made over the course of just this chapter. Right now is the perfect time to silence the noise and strengthen the signal. Revisit the Hustle-isms from the start of Focus & Prioritization.

Reframe the -isms that got you stuck and trade them out for empowering statements to shift your mindset and strengthen your commitment to a more balanced and intentional life.

FOCUS & PRIORITIZATION: REFRAME

	From Hustle-ism... *Why am I so stressed all the time?*	To ANTI-Hustle-ism... *I'm in my flow state, my comfort zone*
1.	Even though you don't have time... "Sure, I have time", "Yeah, I can make that happen", "No, it's not a bad time", "I can take that on"	
2.	"I'm running a little late from a few things that got pushed back this morning, can we push our call 15-30 min?"	
3.	"There's so much on my plate right now, I have no idea what to do 1st"	
4.	"My calendar is stacked, I'll have to push this to next week."	
5.	"If you could just give me one second before we get started, I just need to take care of a few things really quickly."	

NEXT STEPS

You just ANTI-Hustled your way through Chapter 3!

ΔΔΔ

REMEMBER

Return to the **Self Assessment**, again and again, to reassess your growth on the ANTI-Hustle journey

Each time, record the date, individual segment scores, and the **Total Balance Factor** to map your progress

ONWARD

1. Go back and check your scores on **Self-Assessment**
2. Identify which segment & chapter you prioritized up next
3. Head there and dig in where it matters most, ANTI-Hustler

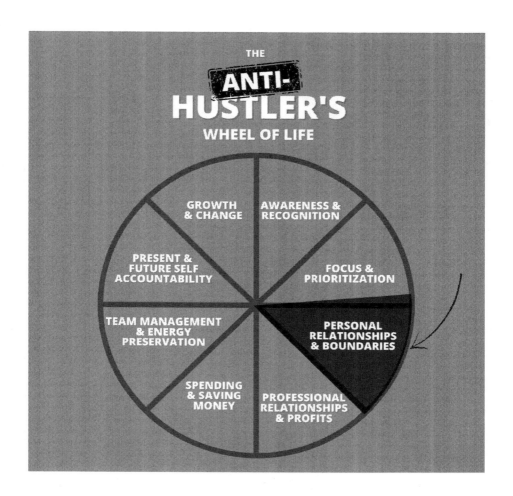

— CHAPTER 04 —
PERSONAL RELATIONSHIPS & BOUNDARIES

FOUNDATION

∆∆∆

The Hustle guru himself, Grant Cardone, once quipped:

"If I was making $400k/year, I would be embarrassed with myself as a husband, as a father, basically as a human being."

Whether you've heard the quote before or not, the sentiment might resonate with you as it often does with entrepreneurs, who sometimes go so far as to quietly nod in agreement.

You may have even been struck with your own ironic epiphany at the dinner table:

"Isn't the whole purpose of my work to be able to have more time with my family and to focus on them more?"

Yet mere moments before…

> Physically, you were sitting there with your family, only to realize you weren't actually there. You were in hustle-la-la-land daydreaming about your business responsibilities instead of being present.

Do you know *what* you missed?

Do you know *that* you're missed?

Does this happen to you *often*?

If you're nodding your head in agreement, no doubt more than a few Hustle-isms have kept you up at night.

Start by returning to what tripped you up in the first place — the Hustle-isms you heard or said for this chapter.

Remember, we're not reinventing the wheel here, it's just another way to sniff out hustle culture where it hides best — in plain sight.

PERSONAL RELATIONSHIPS & BOUNDARIES

- *"I know it's important to you, and I said that I would, but I just can't '___'. But I'm gonna make it happen 'next time'"*
- *"I spend more time at work than I do at home"*
- *"This is my work wife/work husband"*
- *"Listen, what's your problem? You know how much pressure I'm under with this big deadline"*
- *"I'm sorry it took so long to get back to you"*

Cognitive dissonance is a mental conflict that occurs when your beliefs don't line up with your actions.

When that happens, you exist in a state of tension while your brain tries to work out how to resolve the whole misunderstanding.

You can work it out by…

- modifying your thoughts on the matter
- modifying your actions to match your thoughts
- agreeing to disagree… *with yourself*

That last option, despite sounding totally bonkers, happens far more frequently than you might imagine.

It might be happening to you right now.

Take, for example, the common closely held belief that nothing is more important than your partner and family, but there you are at the dinner table not thinking about your family.

That is *if* you end up at the dinner table at all.

What happens when actions don't match up with core values? How do you reconcile the differences in what you say and do?

This isn't a unique problem, but it is a complicated one.

A mind is a complicated machine. Strong, resilient, and entirely capable of playing tricks on a person, the same person with the mind playing tricks. *It's outrageous, really.*

How many times have you been totally convinced the long hours and time away from your family is just sometimes what's necessary for the *benefit of your family?*

One time? Many times? Every time? *Whatever it takes*, right?

It's not entirely your fault.

Hustle culture is more than happy to remind you to acquire and then *acquire more* if you want to adequately provide for your family. You have to be willing to make sacrifices for the people you love to be deserving of their love.

Ironically, hustle culture is also happy to remind you that if you aren't willing to make sacrifices for your business, you aren't deserving of success.

Someone's not telling the whole truth here, and the name rhymes with *Schustle Schulture*. Whether or not I tell you it's malarkey won't matter as much as when you work it out for yourself to reconcile the dissonance.

As you continue to work out the divide between what you believe or don't believe and if your actions line up or don't, you're at ongoing tension with yourself.

What about where two identities of the same person meet?

Fuhgeddaboudit — next stop dissonance central!

If you aren't sure if you've had this experience, it's akin to the great misfortune of the first time you ever saw a teacher outside of the classroom as a kid — mind blown.

It's that same kind of eerie disconnect and tension and disorientation times way too many.

Does not compute.

△△△

The intersection of your identities is filled with tension, incongruency, and imbalance. Who you are in business and who you are in your personal relationships can cause you to rip at the seams.

Even if you can reconcile your identities and manage to keep everything else out of dissonance, being an entrepreneur is still hard on personal relationships.

It's challenging to hold yourself accountable in your personal life the way you would in business.

The focus is on numeric metrics for success, and it's not an option to binge-watch Breaking Bad instead of dealing with the problem.

MINDSET

△△△

Whether or not you think that metrics take the warmth and personality and spontaneity out of relationships, or it feels judgy, etc., you should know that however you decide to reinvest in your personal relationships is exactly what you make it.

I'm not making a 'have the day you deserve' comment but rather a 'make sure you have the right tool for the job'.

And it's not just for romantic relationships.

Defining parameters and needs and wants is a great inventory to take for your family and friends too.

Alternately, Hustle Culture celebrates no accountability, boundaries, and the whatever it takes mentality.

There, you can look forward to…

- pulling all-nighters, and all-dayers
- working on the weekends, all of them
- taking sales meetings in the queue at Disney
- calls outside your parents' at a big family dinner
- feeling guilty more often than not

But are those "the perks" you want?

Freeing up your head space will help calm and focus your attention on the task at hand. The Brain Dump lets you know that work is here and now, for now.

That said, it's time.

The ANTI-Hustle BRAIN DUMP

1. Grab your handy dandy ANTI-Hustler's Companion Handbook at https://antihustlehandbook.com/toolbox
2. Flip to the Brain Dump Prompt for Chapter 4:
   Where in your life does business take priority over family or personal time?

Hold the phone — remember honesty is key here... the answer should not and will not ever honestly be:

> "Business never takes priority over family."

That's an untruth. It's just a bald-faced, bold-faced, and bald-headed lie. Everyone has to negotiate time between areas of their life in different seasons.

Depending on what's happening, sacrificing some amount of personal or family time in order to accomplish business goals is bound to happen.

The goal of this chapter is to find an appropriate and healthy balance that works for you, specifically.

To do that, you have to know where the starting line is for you to set a finish line that's impactful and doable for you. Being an ethereal being that is without mistake or misgiving won't set the lines.

3. Put 10 minutes on the clock, and start writing!
4. Do the thing and once the timer dings, continue reading below with newfound clarity.

Hey, *look at you* — more clarity by the minute.

The reality is, without setting boundaries (and implementing the necessary systems and processes for accountability), entrepreneurs will continue to prove — as they have time and time again — that overworking, creating unnecessary anxiety, and ultimately burning out is their modus operandi.

> *Why is it the go-to if the obvious end result will be burnout? Doesn't that sound just like hustle culture?*

It's the first go-to because in order to have achieved any sort of substantial financial success, there is a high likelihood that significant sacrifices were required on the way up.

As much of a bummer as it is, the significant sacrifices usually fall into the 'personal relationships' bucket. It's not uncommon to find that family, friends, parents, early dating relationships and later failed marriages are the first to go on the chopping block.

But, those sacrifices also likely yielded financial results.

Thus conditioning led to specific expectations: the only way to continue your financial climb is to continue sacrificing your precious personal time.

Something is taken away each time, but then you are also rewarded, which makes it seem like the sacrifice is "worth it."

Because of this conditioning, tangible fear can manifest from nowhere during quality time with friends and family. It boils down to your self-worth now being tied to your productivity — another *"perk."*

Now, "downtime" also feels counter-productive because just sitting around = wasting time. Add *engaging with a potential sacrifice,* and it feels like you're actively playing with fire.

But here's the reality…

Your business likely originated as a way for you to achieve financial freedom AND time freedom.

Yet, so often the latter goal is forgotten for the money.

Money is what people want to talk about so the spotlight manages to stay firmly planted there. Time never really gets its due. I wonder why that is... (cough, hustle, cough-cough, culture).

Moreover, time is not a shared value like money, surprisingly.

You can't safely go into a conversation about how you're really L.I.V.I.N.G. because you only work 3 days a week since your systems are optimized, and your business can run without you.

Someone will equate that to bad, lazy, or stupid.

On the other hand, when it's about money, it's different even if *the numbers* are the same.

If you go into the conversation with how your systems are optimized, note the business can run without you, and mention that your revenue also increased 25% from last quarter... *(unspoken: which is why you can only work the 3 days and offer flexible scheduling)*, someone is already filming the dang biopic.

"Time is money" can't be unheard.

It might even be a hustle-ism, but still, it's not prioritized the same, and that's where hustle does the old divide and conquer on your goals.

The good news?

No matter how deeply ingrained hustle culture is in your life, rest assured there are still plenty of ways out.

ACTION

△△△

Now it's time to take action to quiet the Hustle-isms.

What do you think about an option for 15 minutes of unbridled power?

The ANTI-Hustle RELATIONSHIP LIFE CYCLE AUDIT

To continue enhancing the positive progress in your personal relationships, it's critical to first take stock of where you stand.

The purpose of this audit is to identify which steps you can take to enrich your relationships. If it feels unfamiliar, you're certainly not alone.

It's not a common practice for almost anyone, let alone entrepreneurs, to make a note to audit their relationships properly.

Why not? The resistance is two-fold:

Time. Evaluating, synthesizing, negotiating, planning, and implementing can be time-consuming without systems that work for you in place. It's a hard sell when it takes even more time away from your business.

Truth. No one wants to audit their relationship and learn that there is no relationship. Despite the audit being valuable for enriching your relationship, the ears are still hearing *"audit"* but thinking *"judging"* and *"grading"* and *"failing."*

It's also difficult to move forward in a constructive way when you learn what you need to do to enrich your relationship, but no one is willing to do the work.

Cognitive dissonance strikes again.

△△△

The chart on the following page is quite simple, but holds within it, the unbridled power to truly change the trajectory of your life and business.

No joke.

Keep in mind as you work through this exercise, it is vital to:

- be honest
- give yourself grace
- give yourself more grace
- and give yourself grace again

What's the deal with all the grace, right?

This is work. It's 15 minutes of work.

It's unbridled power for real.

It's the real-real.

You're gonna learn some things, and you might have big feelings about what you learn.

You might also experience cognitive dissonance, wherein what you learn doesn't line up with what you thought you were doing.

Take the necessary time to rectify these relationships.

There are a few really constructive ways to work through the big feelings if you take action to quiet the Hustle-isms.

- As you learn more about the past, you can always choose to leave the past right where it is — behind you. And, you can put those big feelings there too.

    Today you're a person who knows more things than the past person. Acknowledge the big feelings, honor them, use them to inform better decisions from now on, then say goodbye... *because the past is the past.*

- You can take the necessary time to move *forward* in the relationships you value. If the past is the past, it can't be the future too. Leave the band-aids for big feelings in the past and focus on the actions you need to take to rectify your relationships: apologies are just empty words if you're sorry for the same thing twice and you knew it hurt the first time.

    The hustle is a sucker for empty words — like, the biggest fan. And real apologies are best reserved for accidents, slip-ups, and things that you don't intend to repeat because you're aware of the damage caused. So if you do choose to say, *I'm sorry*, the best way to say it will be with your actions.

- A very good way to work through your big feelings, what you learn in the 15-minute audit, and how best to move forward to repair and restore your relationships, is to communicate with the very people you value most in your life.

    Big feelings are hard, and you deserve grace as you progress, no matter what you learn — plus, that was the past. Be kind to yourself now, and know you are taking a critical and positive step in your ANTI-Hustle journey.

As my wife, Shira says,

"Put down the bat, and pick up the feather."

△△△

Now, back to *The Relationship Life Cycle*, the actual doing!

There are 4 possible stages for every relationship: **Accelerating, Booming, Decelerating, or Tanking.**

The 4 stages offer unique insight into patterns and trends within personal relationships. Very luckily for entrepreneurs, no matter how dire the state may seem, relationships are almost always rectifiable.

The 4 Possible Stages of Every Relationship

1. **Accelerating**: Oftentimes a new relationship, but not exclusively, is on the cusp of something grand, and has been pushed into a very exciting time ripe with opportunity by some catalyst, stimulus, action, or event.

2. **Booming:** The metaphorical peak of this relationship has been eclipsed, and now exists 'in the zone', every interaction is exemplary of thriving in a flow state trending upwards.

3. **Decelerating:** A bump in the road — some specific action, nonspecific inaction, or complacency — has changed the trajectory of this relationship trending downwards.

4. **Tanking:** The neglect of this relationship has brought us to the brink. Will it remain in tanking purgatory, be eliminated for good, or is this an opportunity to intervene?

△△△

Before taking action, there's only one more piece of the *Relationship Life Cycle* that you need to learn now that you know how to read it:

How to plot the current landscape.

You will always be able to find a fresh copy of the plot at https://antihustlehandbook.com/toolbox if you don't want to or can't add it to your book right now. Otherwise, write on…

The first step is to identify the most important relationships in your life and choose the ones you would like to include in this audit.

Don't make it too tough - no one will publish this list.

There are truly no right or wrong relationships to include or exclude and no limit to the number of relationships you can utilize.

Seriously, if you're that into it, you can always print more graphs to plot all the relationships you have.

For example, a solid start might be your...

- partner/wife/husband
- parents
- siblings
- three closest friends
- pet

Just look at each relationship there, individually, and based on your first gut reaction, plot it on the chart.

Avoid the tricks your mind may play on you:

> "That relationship isn't that important."

> OR

> "We can't possibly be tanking right now."

None of that. There are no tricks.

Just pick the most important relationships. Choose which to plot. Read on for more instructions. — easy peasy.

∆∆∆

Before plotting your relationship landscape...

Even though we defined each of the 4 quadrants, they are still mostly ambiguous to customize the audit for you. You have the power to define nuances in your plotting, *like in your life.*

- For example, if you have two relationships plotted in *Deceleration*, that doesn't necessarily mean
    - A) you value these relationships equally, or
    - B) these relationships are decelerating equally
- It can mean C.) OTHER — whatever is relevant to you
- If you plot a relationship in *Booming*, you might desire that it STAYS IN BOOMING after 90 days — check
- For the greatest impact, after completing the Relationship Life Cycle Audit, add support. Put reminders on your calendar in increments or just after 90 days when you're ready to re-plot your relationships on a new graph to review your progress.

You're learning things and making progress so remember to extend grace to yourself along the way.

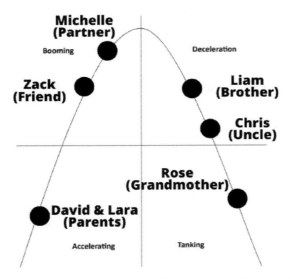

EX. Plotting Relationships for the Relationship Life Cycle in Action

Now it's your turn...

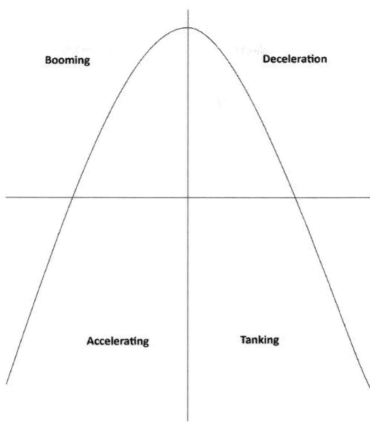

NOTES

The ANTI-Hustle Relationship Life Cycle Audit

1. What relationship did you choose to plot?

ex: Rose, my Grandmother

2. What quadrant did you plot your relationship in?

ex: Tanking

3. Why? What characteristics does your relationship share with the quadrant it's plotted in?

ex: My Grandmother is 90 years old and I haven't spoken to her in over 6 months. I recognize that time with her is likely limited, and if I don't make the time to communicate, I may not have that chance again.

4. Ideally, where would you like to plot this relationship 90 days from now? Why?

ex: At the least, I'd like to move this relationship to Accelerating in the next 90 days. I never planned to neglect this relationship, it just happened over time. I don't want to regret missing out on conversations or having her share her wisdom.

5. What actions will you commit to in the coming days, weeks, and months to ensure you move this relationship to the desired section?

ex: I will commit to calling her today to set a time and date for us to have dinner together. I will make the 3-hour drive to her home in order to spend time with her to enrich this relationship.

6. 90-day progress update...?

ex: I committed to making the call to spend time with Grandma Rose. She was ecstatic that I called and since we talked for an hour, obviously it meant more than I realized. We also met for dinner twice at her house. We arranged to stay with the kids at a hotel in town and stayed the whole weekend. As far as really communicating care and value to her, I think that has been mended, but will require ongoing regular maintenance.

The results will also be indicative of an important reminder: sacrifice is occasionally a negotiated term for every area of your life, depending on the season.

Sacrificing only your personal relationships *consistently* is not a prerequisite to your success and often does not point to larger or lasting success — something will always be missing from the foundation.

Setting boundaries is not only important but it is impossible to prioritize yourself, your family, and your friends without doing so.

Unfortunately, that's just part of the wrecking ball that hustle culture brings to the knife fight.

Actually doing it and being accountable will be the impetus for your greatest success yet.

Until then, maybe just set a starter boundary about refraining from trying to optimize everything in your life for your business. Just go a little easier on that for everyone's sake, *including yours*.

If you care about the true freedom that being an entrepreneur grants you, then don't neglect the time part. Hustle-ism or not, it's the flip end of the money.

You can save it, spend it, and I'm really rooting for you to double your returns in smart investments with the most substantial ROI, like your personal relationships.

And I know your loved ones are too.

TOOLS & RESOURCES

∆∆∆

Access ALL the resources in this chapter and more at:
https://antihustlehandbook.com/toolbox

1. **Love Languages:** Knowing and effectively utilizing Gary Chapman's 5 love languages will deeply impact your relationships

2. **Get To, Have To, Want To:** A 3-step journal to help classify your actions in relation to those around you

3. **Why Have I Not Done X?:** So often we procrastinate on things we want to do with our loved ones. Why?

THE CLOSER
THE REFRAMING TECHNIQUE

△△△

Before you go, really reflect on the progress you've made over the course of just this chapter. Revisit the negative statements from the start of Personal Relationships & Boundaries.

Right now is the perfect time to silence the noise and reframe the -isms that got you stuck to begin with.

Trade them out for empowering statements that will help you shift your mindset and strengthen your commitment to a more balanced and intentional life.

	PERSONAL RELATIONSHIPS & BOUNDARIES: REFRAME	
	From Hustle-ism... *Why am I so stressed all the time?*	**To ANTI-Hustle-ism...** *I'm in my flow state, my comfort zone*
1.	"I know it's important to you and I said that I would, but I just can't __. I'll make it happen next time though."	
2.	"I spend more time at work than I do at home."	
3.	"This is my work wife/husband."	
4.	"Listen, what's your problem? You know how much pressure I'm under with this big deadline."	
5.	"I'm sorry it took so long to get back to you."	

NEXT STEPS

You just ANTI-Hustled your way through Chapter 4!

∆∆∆

REMEMBER

Return to the **Self Assessment**, again and again, to reassess your growth on the ANTI-Hustle journey

Each time, record the date, individual segment scores, and the **Total Balance Factor** to map your progress

ONWARD

1. Go back and check your scores on **Self-Assessment**

2. Identify which segment & chapter you prioritized up next

3. Head there and dig in where it matters most, ANTI-Hustler

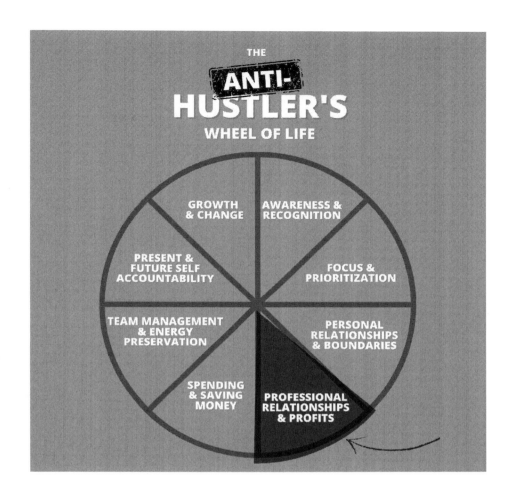

— CHAPTER 05 —

PROFESSIONAL RELATIONSHIPS & PROFITS

FOUNDATION

△△△

How many times have you heard this one?

"Your network is your net worth."

One? Two? Three million times?

Fair enough.

It's as cliché as can be, so you can roll your eyes for the 3 millionth time, but that won't make it any less true.

Network is the first thing that comes up in this chapter for a very good reason and in the very right place — it's foundational to your success, regardless of your industry, niche, field, or business classification.

The way you build professional relationships and with whom you build them creates a crucial and indispensable network of support.

It's *made of actual people* who are there to give you a leg up when you're staring down the most difficult challenges in your business.

If that's so, then why are you still hearing the same static blocking your signals for success?

Start by reviewing what got you here so you can make a plan to get out of here: check out where your clarity is clouded, and the Hustle-isms drown out the sweet sounds of success.

PROFESSIONAL RELATIONSHIPS & PROFITS

- "I'm just trying to squeeze as much money as I can out of him/her"

- "I'm struggling to manage all of these opportunities. There's just too much to do"

- "I've been working on this big deal for months! Is this thing ever going to actually close?!?"

- "[Competitor] just got lucky, they didn't even have to work for it"

- "I hate dealing with [client], but I need the money"

Still hearing them? *But, have you reached out to anyone in your network that could help? Surely, there's someone…*

- Have you tried contacting your mentor, their mentor, or the lady they go to who does hypnotherapy?

- What about the dog-psychic guy, or the couple from the old neighborhood who retired before you started in business?

- Did you message the real estate mogul from back home you went to college with? Not Bernard, the other one — Leonard or was it Lawrence?

- What about your old boss from the concession stands or that podcast guy you love so much — or is he a vlogger? Have you tried talking to your dad about it?

Networks are far-reaching support channels that can match needs to resources in record time, but is that enough for you? In a society that desires, *if not requires* instant gratification, anything that takes longer than 10 minutes is newly irrelevant.

- At the 5-minute mark, even delivery of the "desired result" has already become a nuisance. Unsubscribe.

- At 3 minutes, *shaking your head in disbelief*, you take whatever you came for and rush away.

Relationships, particularly professional relationships but not exclusively, have managed to convert from something priceless to dollars and cents.

This is the calling card for the nefarious work of hustle culture!

Look closely, and you'll recognize it in any one of the literal hundreds of thousands of books on how to 'do' professional relationships right.

You must do relationships like any other successful transaction: optimizing them, then maximizing them.

Another translation: *How to squeeze the most value from your network and other weird things that you should not do because human relationships are not the same as systems.*

In theory, the core tenets of optimization and maximization are incredibly valuable for systems and processes.

For these purposes, any human being - let alone entrepreneurs - will benefit from the outcomes of optimized business operations. However, it's not meant for every situation, even if amazing.

This is the same basic principle behind ketchup use, right? It doesn't have to get weird, there's no reason for it to get weird, yet people will make it so weird, so fast, and so often.

Ever heard of ketchup on pizza? *Yea, me neither.*

The unrelenting push to over-optimize anything and everything also creates anxiety, stress, and so much *frustration* that it ultimately leads straight to burnout — an outcome so predictable the path is clear-cut and worn.

If optimization was meant to make things better, faster, and more... how do you keep arriving back at burnout?

MINDSET

△△△

Freeing up your head space will help calm and focus your attention on the task at hand.

The Brain Dump lets you know that work is here and now, for now.

That said, *it's time.*

The ANTI-Hustle BRAIN DUMP

1. Grab your handy dandy ANTI-Hustler's Companion Handbook at https://antihustlehandbook.com/toolbox

2. Flip to the Brain Dump Prompt for Chapter 5:
   Think fast. What are the 5 most important professional relationships in my life right now? Why?

3. Put 10 minutes on the clock, and start writing!

4. Do the thing and once the timer dings, continue reading below with newfound clarity.

Hey, *look at you* — more clarity by the minute, but what good has playing favorites ever done?

It's called allocating your resources wisely — *ever heard of it?*

Knowing your most important human resources is a helpful inventory to have just like any other resource.

Aside from monetary investments, you're also more willing to invest time and effort into the relationships that best support you and your growth as a human and business owner.

Even then, deciding how to choose which relationships to invest more or less in and how to best allocate your top resources is still tricky.

These kinds of processes were made for inhuman things, not for head and heart systems with human things like feelings.

Ultimately, you have to decide for yourself...

What makes a relationship the most profitable to me?

- immediate financial return
- invaluable wisdom from sages
- long-term financial stability
- paths to shortcut goals
- mentors with all the right words
- unconditional acceptance and support
- referral partners that expand connections

Hustle Culture maintains that it is 100% possible to optimize and maximize *every. single. professional. relationship.*

You don't have to choose, and you can simply weed out the least profitable on the way to the top, wherever that is.

It is most certainly *not possible* to nurture and maximize in this manner.

Moreover, word to the wise, you should never weed out people by how profitable or not profitable they are or are not.

None of those things are reasonable.

To consider relationships that don't impact the bottom line immediately as *'necessary to cut out of your life'*, positions human beings as just weapons on a financial toolbelt ready to be wielded at a moment's notice.

Treating people like financial assets and reducing them to dollar and cent amounts is not a great way to expand your network.

People are not going to respond well to that.

Further, when entrepreneurs try optimizing and maximizing everything, especially very hastily, ultimately things fall apart.

> Besides, just how many metaphorical balls do you think you can actually juggle?
>
> Honestly, it works literally, too — you probably can't physically juggle more than 5 balls at once.
>
> *Keep in mind, the WORLD RECORD is 14 balls.*
>
> And you have a lot more relationships to juggle than 14…

The ultimate goal of this chapter is to prioritize and maximize the right relationships.

This goal is underscored by the idea that you don't have to feel bad about what you can't do because you seriously can't do everything.

ΔΔΔ

Take Rick, *the person I just made up for this scenario,* who is making his way in the world the best he knows how. He's living and learning about the same *Professional Relationships & Profits* landscape as everyone else here…

- Rick is part of a religious community with over 100 families, many of which own small businesses that Rick can offer marketing services.
- Rick is a preferred partner of a Dental franchise that has over 75 locations. He currently provides marketing services to 13 locations.
- Rick is part of his Alumni network at his Alma Mater.
- Rick sponsors the events of a CRM company that his ideal clients use.

Wow. Okay, Rick. We see you!

The question is, will Rick see how best to allocate his resources?

Do you think he will see ways to optimize and maximize, given his current set-up?

Why or why not?

With his four professional relationships and networks, how **should** Rick choose to spend his time? How **would you** invest in these relationships to maximize the opportunities?

It's very tempting to say, Rick can do it all! In a vacuum, it's feasible to consider Rick could manage it all — he seems like he's got it going on.

After you figure in all of Rick's personal & professional obligations and add in the current responsibilities he has tied to ongoing relationships already, Rick seems like he might have *too much going on.*

Things might slip through the cracks without him knowing.

Then what?

Hustle culture screams for Rick to wake up earlier and work later. Screaming that he's a fool, not for taking on too much, but for not cloning himself to be in six places at once.

Yelling to the skies, No-win-Rick never even learned basic DNA replication or gene expression and now no one can have nice things. Team Rick failed yet again, hustle culture screams.

Worst of all?

Whenever you have the same amorphous *"hustle culture screaming at me"* nightmare, it's always just actually you screaming at you — your own mini-me is the hustle harpy.

ACTION

△△△

With that in mind, it's time to take action to quiet the Hustle-isms — no matter where they come from.

Let's start with a strong footing: acceptance. This is not accepting that you're a failure. This is an acceptance that you need to expand your options.

Here it is: You won't be able to perfectly maximize and/or optimize all of your professional relationships. I said it. I meant it. It's true. And that's okay!

If you haven't already, know you will absolutely drop the ball on at least one - and likely far more than one - potentially valuable relationship(s) over the years.

Admittedly, it won't be great, but it will be okay...

- When you forget to follow up on time
- When you have to choose between two
- When you lose a valuable team member *(see CH. 7)*
- When you figure out you've invested unwisely

The key to ANTI-Hustling your way to the right professional relationships is evaluating your options, so that you can clearly plan out a course of action that will benefit you most.

So, how do you maximize your professional relationships without spreading yourself too thin? *Asking for a friend...*

The SWOT Analysis

SWOT is an acronym that stands for Strengths, Weaknesses, Opportunities, and Threats.

You'll find the following SWOT template at https://antihustlehandbook.com/toolbox, so you can fill it out as you read through this chapter.

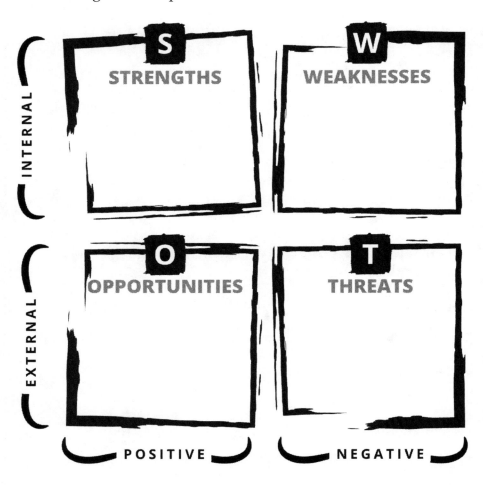

Notice how Strengths and Weaknesses are marked as "Internal" while Opportunities and Threats are listed as "External." These markers are used to clearly differentiate between any potential similarities in the quadrants.

For simplicity's sake, you can define "Internal" as something you have within your control and "External" as something outside of your control. Use the SWOT Analysis below to take stock of your Professional Relationships.

S = Strengths

What relationships are the strongest for you right now?

- Perhaps it's your supportive business partner?
- Is it a mentor who guided you to achieve your goals?
- Has a referral partner sent you an influx of business?

List 3 or more strong relationships, & consider the prompt:

-
-
-

Prompt: *How can I nurture these relationships to maintain or even increase their impact in my life?*

NOTES

W = Weakness

What relationships are the weakest for you right now?

- Is your team strained because you're micro-managing?
- Do you lack mentorship or guidance?
- Are you struggling with an affiliate partner?

List out at least 3 weak relationships that you'd like to improve, and then consider the following prompt...

-
-
-

Prompt: *How can I nurture these relationships over the next 30 days in order to move them into the STRENGTHS category?*

NOTES

O = Opportunities

What relationships have the most opportunity to bring you closer to your defined version of success and happiness?

- Could a new hire help grow your business?
- Met a referral partner that's potentially impactful?
- Someone you look up to that could be a mentor?

List out at least 3 opportunistic relationships that you'd like to act upon, and then consider the following prompt...

•

•

•

Prompt: *How can I capitalize on these opportunities in the next 30 days to move them into the STRENGTHS category?*

NOTES

T = Threats

What relationships are threatening to damage your life?

- Competitor who is undercutting you?
- Disgruntled past client giving you a bad rap?
- Former business partner threatening legal action?

List out at least 3 threatening relationships that you need to act upon, and then consider the following prompt…

-
-
-

Prompt: *What uncomfortable actions are required to ensure strained relationships are no longer a threat in 3 months?*

NOTES

_____

_____

_____

_____

_____

_____

_____

_____

The SWOT analysis can be done at any time in your life, but is especially effective when you feel the weight of all the professional relationships you're managing.

Try it monthly, quarterly, annually, or whenever you feel the need to clarify your current relationships.

Do you want the skeleton key for making the SWOT the most useful and most powerful it can be? It's simple — TAKE ACTION

If you only take stock of your relationships but take no action, nothing will change. If you take action but have no idea what your purpose is, something might change but it's really a wildcard — could be good, could be bad, could be useful.

Better yet, that kind of confusion and waste of resources could be avoided entirely by doing both: taking stock and *taking action.*

Action with purpose will always provide better results than hustling for the sake of hustling. *Always.*

Remember those who are rewarded for the journey aren't necessarily doing more or working harder. They simply did a better job at evaluating the landscape, making a plan, acting upon it, and reaping the rewards.

That's the ANTI-Hustle way.

TOOLS & RESOURCES

∆∆∆

Access ALL the resources in this chapter and more at:
https://antihustlehandbook.com/toolbox

1. **ERAM:** A tool to ensure you and your team are on the same page and what's needed to bolster their effectiveness *(See CH. 7)*

2. **Love languages:** Everyone communicates differently. Learning the love languages of your personal and professional contacts will enrich your relationships with them

3. **Enneagram:** A personality system to better understand yourself, your personal relationships, and your professional connections.

THE CLOSER
THE REFRAMING TECHNIQUE

△△△

Before you go, really reflect on the progress you've made over the course of just this chapter. Revisit the Hustle-isms from the start of Professional Relationships & Profits.

Right now is the perfect time to silence the noise and strengthen the signal. Reframe the -isms that got you stuck to begin with.

Trade them out for empowering statements that will help you shift your mindset and strengthen your commitment to a more balanced and intentional life.

	PROFESSIONAL RELATIONSHIPS & PROFITS: REFRAME	
	From Hustle-ism... *Why am I so stressed all the time?*	**To ANTI-Hustle-ism...** *I'm in my flow state, my comfort zone*
1.	"I'm just trying to squeeze as much money as I can out of him/her."	
2.	"I'm struggling to manage all these opportunities. There's just too much to do."	
3.	"I've been working on this big deal for months! Is this thing ever going to actually close?!?"	
4.	"[Competitor] just got lucky, they didn't even have to work for it."	
5.	"I hate dealing with [client], but I need the money."	

NEXT STEPS

You just ANTI-Hustled your way through Chapter 5!

∆∆∆

REMEMBER

Return to the **Self Assessment**, again and again, to reassess your growth on the ANTI-Hustle journey

Each time, record the date, individual segment scores, and the **Total Balance Factor** to map your progress

ONWARD

1. Go back and check your scores on **Self-Assessment**

2. Identify which segment & chapter you prioritized up next

3. Head there and dig in where it matters most, ANTI-Hustler

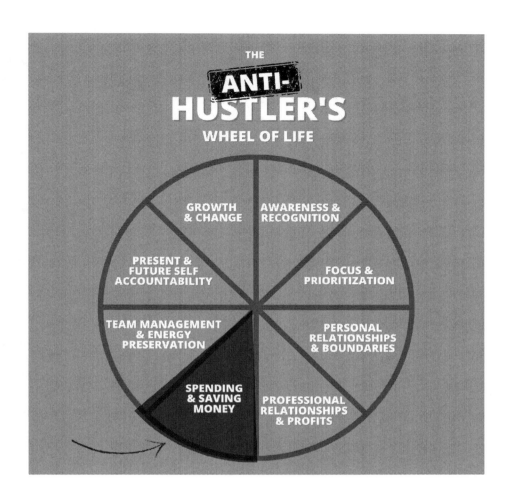

CHAPTER 06

SPENDING & SAVING MONEY

FOUNDATION

△△△

Define for the class: What is **enough** money?

In the world of social media, financial flexing is all the rage. How much money you make — exaggerated or not — is a status symbol of hustle culture success *(or failure)*.

But once your basic needs are met. Once you've developed a 'nest egg', and once you're no longer 'scraping by' paycheck by paycheck…

How do you determine what is enough?

An essential component of hustle *culture* is the never-ending pursuit of the acquisition of wealth, usually in the form of money.

More specifically, and in less office-friendly words, you might say hustle culture is a *zombified* drive to get *more always*.

Another core pillar of hustle culture must be a shared understanding there is *never enough,* and *there never will be enough.*

To get you to jump at the chance for more, hustle culture does a really good job of leading you directly inside your head and trapping you there.

Try these on for size.

- No matter how much money you've acquired, you have an almost instinctual drive to still acquire more.
- *Of course*, you're saving for an unknown future, that's why you're hustling so hard now.

  Of course, you also have no idea how much money to save either, so *"more"* seems like a good place to start… and be *forever*.
- 'Financial freedom' is always at the forefront of your mind but it also always seems to inch further away. Exactly how much is needed for your financial freedom?
- You know the definition — *fulfillment of a need or want, contentment, source or means of enjoyment, gratification* — still, you struggle to decide if satisfaction is a measure you want to live by. Does it feel *limiting*?

The specifics of basic financial fulfillment often go overlooked and undefined by entrepreneurs.

Is it an oversight? Is it by design?

You tell me.

∆∆∆

Think back to what brought you here, all the noise that makes it hard to hear the coins clank, and discern which advice is best on important fiscal affairs, like saving and spending your money wisely.

Money is often an incredibly uncomfortable and sensitive topic for entrepreneurs, right up there with ego.

Don't let bias and bitterness stop you from getting past the hustle blockade on this one.

You got this.

Which Hustle-isms are blocking the sweet sounds of triumph?

SPENDING & SAVING MONEY

- *"No way I have enough money yet — even the average millionaire has AT LEAST 7 streams of income"*
- *Everyone knows you have to… "pay to play, invest to impress, or let your money talk when you walk in a room"*
- *"I'm not exactly sure what my profit is month-over-month. I know it's something I should be more on top of"*
- *"[Competitor] is already at 6 figures per month. Where are MY 6-figures per month?! Let's pivot to what they're doing"*
- *"Cutting staff and salaries are where the real savings are — especially with all this AI, how could you NOT?"*

Money is complicated. The way you talk about money and use money is initially shaped by forces outside your control.

Much like mindset, you have a set of beliefs, attitudes, and thoughts that all shape your perceptions, behaviors, and actions.

The whole thing is social and value-oriented.

When people say "money mindset," it's for sure a hustle-ism.

Regardless, determining WHAT your actual money mindset encompasses, including the potential biases that set up successes or failures, can help build your financial baseline.

For example, you might have been raised in a certain way that forbids the talk of money in polite conversation or alternatively one that promotes financial transparency.

It's just that way sometimes.

But it doesn't have to be that way forever. There are a lot of options to educate yourself on money matters, this is one.

Across every industry, many choices range in content from low to high hustle levels. Money truly only gets a 360° approach once success has already been attained. It's very difficult to go back and translate that experience 1 to 1 — *me after I set out on this venture.*

As a result, people will run to get in line for financial gurus for "the opportunity" to pay and privately inquire in hopes that it will make all the difference in their own entrepreneurial pursuit because… *shaking their head, "I just don't know how you do it."*

But people do it all the time!

They do both equally well: they can expertly manage finances, and they can expertly implode finances.

Some people can manage to squeeze a dollar out of a dime, and others will spend their last dime and finance dimes they don't yet have to frantically grasp at clarity on monetary matters because the sheer amount of information and advice available is enough to make Ben Franklin's head spin.

Two issues further compound the delicate nature of money every time. However, they also can create great opportunities to utilize the power of your network and strong mentors.

1. **Decision overwhelm:** When it comes to managing finances, it's also ridiculously easy to feel overwhelmed by the sheer amount of information and advice available. How do you decide which course is the right course of action? And where do you get the support to stick to it?

2. **Runaway ego:** Sometimes the best way to get to the finish line is from the starting line. No one and I mean no one readily agrees to go back and start from the beginning in order to reach financial goals, but sometimes it's the path of least resistance.

As far as exchange rates go, sometimes the ego is stronger than the dollar.

MINDSET

△△△

Freeing up your head space will help calm and focus your attention on the task at hand. The Brain Dump lets you know that work is here and now, for now. That said, *it's time.*

The ANTI-Hustle BRAIN DUMP

1. Grab your handy dandy ANTI-Hustler's Companion Handbook at https://antihustlehandbook.com/toolbox

2. Flip to the Brain Dump Prompt for Chapter 6:
   What is enough money to you and why?

If you've never done this exercise before, you'll be astonished at how hard you've been working towards an undefined goal.

No one has the right to tell you what is right or wrong.

You don't have to say: "I'll have enough money when I can solve world hunger."

You're STILL allowed to say: "I want enough money to have two Ferraris."

Remember, agency is an entrepreneur's greatest gift.

3. Put 10 minutes on the clock, and start writing!

4. Do the thing and once the timer dings, continue reading below with newfound clarity.

Hey, look at you — more clarity by the minute and newfound financial milestones!

The late great Notorious B.I.G. said it best:

> *"Mo' Money, Mo' Problems"*

Money IS NOT the great panacea hustle culture tells you it is.

Money IS the world's greatest amplifier. If you are…

- Easily stressed, anxious, and impatient, creating more financial wealth will only **amplify your challenges.**
- Generous, selfless, and charitable, having more money will **amplify your impact.**

Before we go any further, please know I love money.

Like, *love love*. From crisp bills that you can fold into neat little squares and sharp-pointed stars, to shiny coins that clink and clank in your pocket and get flipped for dinner or dares, and, more so, to the alluring promise of long-term financial security.

So, I had an unhealthy relationship with money for a while.

Mostly because I bought into the idea early that *just a little bit more* money would fix my problems.

But that's the whole thing with *just a little bit more*.

There will always be more out there. The problem is in thinking that every opportunity out there is yet another opportunity for you to acquire a *little more*.

It's what Michael Scott said that Wayne Gretzky said that keeps hustlers up at night…

> *"You miss 100% of the shots you don't take."*

The heat is on. The pressure is high. Gotta take the shots. 110%.

Hustlers take it to heart, and they let it set them apart by moving the goalposts anytime a financial milestone is achieved — *for more.*

When it's close to meeting the mark, you'll inexplicably raise the bar *just a little bit more* each time.

At first glance, this might not seem like a bad thing, but "just *a little bit more*" is a moving target, AKA a goal with no clear definition, and it inherently has a 0% chance of success.

Without success or achievement, an entrepreneur shifts into burnout, crises, and dissatisfaction.

No matter how much money has been accumulated, it's not enough because it's never the "right" amount.

Of course it isn't right, you changed the "goal" again last week.

There's a better way.

ACTION

△△△

Go back to your notes for the Brain Dump in this chapter, **What is enough money to you and why?**

Give it a glance.

How did you come to it?

Do you have a system in place?

Do you have an actual number? Is the number calculated or is it arbitrary — "when I'm a bazillionaire!"

Think about the level of agency you have regarding your happiness and goals.

△△△

When you nudge hustle culture out of the spotlight and start determining for yourself *'What is enough?'* — *not just more forever* — What can that look like? How can you get there?

Do you know?

When you give this work the time and dedication to figure it out, then set numbers and goals, something good happens.

Defining goals and setting purpose sets up option upon option upon option upon option — *an abundance of options, okay?* — to expand before you.

For instance, as far as ways to get to specific numbers and financial goals, you can **X START RIGHT HERE** and ANTI-Hustle through the new options below as you wish...

- check out The Success Calculator in this chapter
- The ANTI-Hustler Companion online resources at https://antihustlehandbook.com/toolbox
- don't forget the rest of the ANTI-Hustle chapters
- revisit my PART I: The Hustle narrative at the beginning
- review all the really great resources in the back matter

All those new options just showed up today, and it's just the beginning. Stay on the ANTI-Hustle path, do the work, and see what shows up tomorrow.

But, you didn't pick up the ANTI-Hustler's Handbook just for me to tell you, *"Hey You! Enjoy your ANTI-Hustle journey!"*

Maybe you wanted to go into the tool for Chapter 6 on familiar ground. How about a little reinforcement on what works? Focus on **maximizing profits instead of revenue**.

Try:

- Tracking financial KPIs at home/work for accountability
- Bookkeeping for a real picture of your financial health
- The Define, Design, Do journal for planning in *Chapter 8*
- The tool that is *choice* for **Spending & Saving Money...**

The ANTI-Hustle Success Calculator

The dangers have already been established for what happens when entrepreneurs fail to clarify, *"What exactly is enough money?"*

Not to drive it into the ground, but...

> When the definition of "enough," a marker for your financial success, is allowed the fickle mutability of:
>
> *"I desire financial freedom."*
>
> The definition will always be hustle destitution instead.

It's true, and I don't love that news for you. Though, I do love being the bearer of good news.

Good news: Defining 'enough' just got a whole lot easier if you want to work out a definition and say, "nuh-uh," to hustle destitution.

> All it takes is a calculator...
>
> A Success Calculator, if I may be so bold.
>
> Go grab The ANTI-Hustle Success Calculator in your Companion Handbook at
> https://antihustlehandbook.com/toolbox
>
> Heading over to the Companion Handbook is an ideal way to make big progress here.

Can we talk?

Did you just think, *"I'll grab the success calculator later — I'll just keep reading to get the gist of it."*? Did that happen?

Please consider the ramifications of continuing inaction.

If you're reading this chapter, **you're here for action**. The whole point is about identifying an abundance of options, making smart plans to optimize your happiness and freedom, and then taking purposeful action to make it so.

Go grab the Success Calculator. Make it so.

This is not a place to simply 'read about how the success calculator works'... That won't cut the mustard.

Read about how it works while you're working through it.

I'm glad we talked.

I hope you grabbed the Success Calculator and you're with me now. I want you to get a handle on "enough" because it's past time for you to stop hustling so hard.

ΔΔΔ

The Success Calculator is a spreadsheet that requires your input in order to spit out exactly what you need to live your ideal life. It quite literally has vast power.

The Success Calculator can not only completely change your life but the life of your family, your friends, your team, your clients, and anyone else you directly or indirectly impact.

It is truly that effective. Now it's time to break down the parts of the Success Calculator, check out the steps, and learn to wield its power!

The ANTI-Hustle Success Calculator
STEP 1: INTERPRETATION

A standard definition of interpretation is 'the action of explaining the meaning of something', and, for the success calculator specifically, it's to give you the freedom to feel comfortable coloring outside the lines.

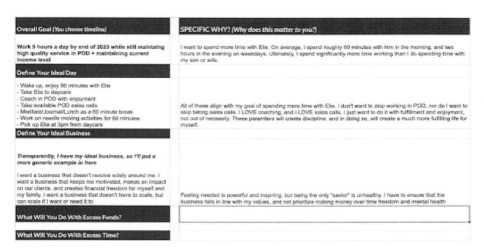

Grab Your Copy at *https://antihustlehandbook.com/toolbox*

CAUTION: The compulsion will be strong to answer the prompts with your standard mindset traps intact: hustle biases, societal constraints, your parent's definition of success, #MOREmoneymindset, comparison, and other innumerable factors pushing or pulling you to do things.

Try to get outside of those traps before beginning. This is *your* interpretation, *your* win you're working to define.

IN THE INTERPRETATION SECTION, you'll find 5 prompts that will allow for infinite flexibility and empower you to radically define the life you want to live:

- What is your overall goal? *(You choose the timeline)*
- Define your ideal day
- Define your ideal business
- What will you do with excess funds?
- What will you do with excess time?

CAUTION: If you do not spend the appropriate time working through these 5 prompts — that is, the only action you take is to *avoid defining your ideal life (inaction)* — you are guaranteed to have someone else define it for you.

Plenty of people would be more than happy to do that for you. Your clients, your peers, your friends, your family, your team, your community, and anyone and EVERYONE else will always…

- want to give their "perfect plan" for you
- want to fill your calendar with responsibilities
- want to add more to your to-do list
- want to ensure a piece of you for them

Just take the time to answer the prompts.

Then you can also take comfort in knowing that you're making mammoth progress toward living YOUR best life — truly what ANTI-Hustling is all about.

The ANTI-Hustle Success Calculator:
STEP 2: FINANCIAL DESIGN

With newfound clarity on what exactly constitutes your ideal life and business, the work is to define exactly what enough money is for you to LIVE your ideal life.

Check out the box in the top left corner that says, *"90-Day Financial Goal"*. To make financial goals more attainable, 90 days is a good mark, but changing it won't in any way affect the calculator. Next, you will be prompted to fill out your personal monthly expenses alongside anything else you'd like to purchase.

For **annual expenses**, divide the costs by 12 and use that information for a more accurate picture of monthly expenses.

Then, as a play on the "saving for a rainy day" cliché, the calculator multiplies monthly expenses by 1.5x to ensure you have more than enough excess to get through any situation.

AT LONG LAST your "Total $$$ Needed For Ideal Life" will be automatically calculated:

Grab Your Copy at https://antihustlehandbook.com/toolbox

(monthly expenses)(1.5) + (your desired purchases)

The number that spits out at G2 is your **defined win** — that number is your goal. Your "enough" has just been defined.

SPENDING & SAVING MONEY | 225

CONGRATS!

You just ANTI-Hustled Your Way Through Defining "Enough"

△△△

And perhaps, for the first time in your entrepreneurial career, you have a personal financial goal that *means something.*

Most importantly, not only does the number mean *something*, it means something to *you*.

You may be surprised, shocked, underwhelmed — meh, or overwhelmed entirely by the number. Maybe it's lower than you anticipated or potentially far higher than you expected.

No matter the unique number staring at you, remember how powerful it is to have this number in the first place — *for you*.

- No more moving goalposts
- No more other people defining your success
- No more lacking clarity on what is enough
- No more "*just a little bit more*" forever

But I know what you're thinking…

Yes, of course, any number is still capable of being changed at any moment. But now you have more impetus than 'just on a whim'.

And, just like with any well-defined goal, managing the steps to achieve it and tracking progress along the way can provide you with a greater sense of control and motivation.

When you work towards a concrete objective, rather than something subject to how you feel like any old 'Tuesday afternoon when 2 calls up and cancel,' you also have greater control over the consistency of your finances.

Because you've planned for "enough," which includes contingencies, you have the renewed authority to decide on what you spend versus what you save.

The ANTI-Hustle Success Calculator: CONSIDERATIONS FOR SPENDING

Once you've completed the Success Calculator, you're walking tall into part 2 of your entrepreneurial life.

This is uncharted territory.

Here's what I know about new things:

- Even when something is good and exciting and potentially life-changing for the better…
- If there is no support, it's very easy to feel overwhelmed and even easier to give up on the new thing in favor of the familiarity of the old thing
- Therefore, having support is crucial to a person's success in fulfilling their potential
- Please enjoy this book and all the resources that come with it — I am also here as a real human being

Keep the following considerations in mind as you work out how you want to get to where you want to go ("enough").

∆∆∆

I like thinking about "spending" in terms of "investing"

What investments can you make that will free up more of your time in order to get closer to your ideal day?

Strong potential options if it's a fit for your needs:

- hiring a VA to handle your emails and other tasks
- hiring an automation expert to decrease repetition
- hiring a Client Success Manager to scale smoothly

If you're not yet at your financial goal, what investment would create the highest ROI potential for your business?

Strong potential options if it's a fit for your needs:

- any of the hiring/time investments above
- advertising solutions to generate more clients
- coaching or mentorship to accelerate your growth
- sponsorships to generate multiple clients at once

Look at your "Desired Purchases" section and determine if there's anything you can buy now. Why? If you can afford it, don't continually procrastinate spending on what you desire.

That's what money is for… buying stuff. Don't feel bad about it.

Strong reminders to **meet your needs now**… and later:

- ROI isn't just financial earnings or time-saving
- ROI requires and yields from all aspects of life
- ROI is fulfillment, satisfaction, and enjoyment

The ANTI-Hustle Success Calculator:
CONSIDERATIONS FOR SAVING

Keep your eyes on the "Desired Purchases" section. What options do you see in order to start saving today?

For example, if you want to purchase a car or a home and know there's a down payment required,

- Where can you begin saving $100, $250, or even $500 each month right now?

For example, if you have excess funds right now, what can you save for in the future?

- Do you have a retirement plan in place?
- Can you make sure you do and it's optimal?
- Do you have a 529 Savings Plan for the kids?

If you're low on funds, but your expenses are increasingly high, find out what can be cut.

Where and how can you save money right now?

Start by reviewing the "WANT" or "NEED" column and investigate your expenses:

- **Q:** Do you have extraneous personal monthly expenses that are billed monthly?
- **Q:** Do you have business tools not being used that you can cancel or unsubscribe to?
- **Q:** What other expenses can you cut that are not directly related to increasing revenues and profits?

△△△

Remember… whether cutting, adding, buying, saving, or spending, none of it is random anymore.

So before you start slashing or spending, check to ensure:

- Decisions are based on solid data
- Actions have a clear purpose
- Sacrifices are intentional and limited

You are the designer of your dream life, and you earned this.

Make it so.

TOOLS & RESOURCES

ΔΔΔ

Access ALL the resources in this chapter and more at: https://antihustlehandbook.com/toolbox

1. **Define, Design, Do:** A 3-step process to developing a clear action plan to achieve your personal and professional goals (See CH. 8)

2. **Rocketmoney.com:** Formerly Truebill, this app helps you better understand your financial health through tracking your expenses

3. **Revenue Goal Setting Calculator:** How to achieve your business' financial goals through specific monthly actions & KPIs based on your unique offers and pricing

THE CLOSER
THE REFRAMING TECHNIQUE

△△△

Before you go, really reflect on the progress you've made over the course of just this chapter. Revisit the negative statements from the start of Spending & Saving Money. Right now is the perfect time to silence the noise and strengthen the signal. Reframe the -isms that got you stuck to begin with.

Trade them out for empowering statements that will help you shift your mindset and strengthen your commitment to a more balanced and intentional life.

	SPENDING & SAVING MONEY: REFRAME	
	From Hustle-ism... *Why am I so stressed all the time?*	**To ANTI-Hustle-ism...** *I'm in my flow state, my comfort zone*
1.	"No way I have enough money yet — even the average millionaire has AT LEAST 7 streams of income."	
2.	"Everyone knows you have to pay to play, invest to impress, or let your money talk when you enter a room."	
3.	"I'm not exactly sure what my profit is month-over-month. I know it's something I should be more on top of."	
4.	"[Competitor] is already at 6 figures a month. Where are MY 6-figure months?! Let's pivot to what they're doing."	
5.	"Cutting staff and salaries are where the real savings are — especially with all this AI, how could you NOT."	

NEXT STEPS

You just ANTI-Hustled your way through Chapter 6!

△△△

REMEMBER

Return to the **Self Assessment**, again and again, to reassess your growth on the ANTI-Hustle journey

Each time, record the date, individual segment scores, and the **Total Balance Factor** to map your progress

ONWARD

1. Go back and check your scores on **Self-Assessment**

2. Identify which segment & chapter you prioritized up next

3. Head there and dig in where it matters most, ANTI-Hustler

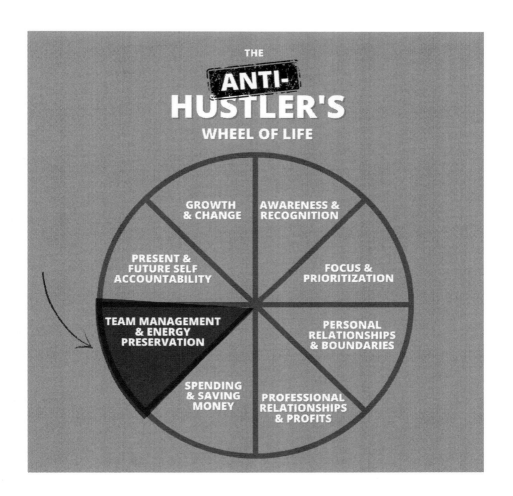

CHAPTER 07

TEAM MANAGEMENT & ENERGY PRESERVATION

FOUNDATION

△△△

Slow your scroll — don't be tempted to skip this one.

If you read the title and thought, **but I already have a team**, or **but I don't even have a team**… *this chapter is still for you, all of you.*

Because it's not *just about the team* or *just about conserving energy*. Although hopefully, you have systems and processes in place for both! If not, this is an even better place to start.

It's really about getting the strongest options in place to edge out the hustle where you think you have it beat. This is where everyone thinks they always have it beat.

Do a quick review of the **Team Management & Energy Preservation Hustle-isms** that make it hard for you to hear the sweet sounds of success.

TEAM MANAGEMENT & ENERGY PRESERVATION

- "My team is not pulling their weight. I'm doing too much!"
- "I can do this faster myself"
- "Only I can do [insert task] correctly"
- "Hiring someone will take too long"
- "If I automate, the tech will break, or something will get lost in the mix. I just know it."

The Hustle and the human ego have been long-time partners, and they'll probably be *'besties for the resties'*.

Together, they create a blinding and insatiable desire to achieve big, hairy, audacious successes with fortunes untold, fame, riches, and notoriety.

Despite *not really knowing what any of that might actually entail*, it's a pursuit that can go sideways very quickly.

∆∆∆

Has anyone ever said to you, hand on hip and head shaking,

> "I just don't know how you do it..."

... and immediately you begin glowing with deep pride as a powerful, yet ominous feeling of superiority washed over you?

That's probably a sign, or it could be any number of other indicators (*you're ignoring*), telling you very plainly your ego is at the wheel and in overdrive.

Not surprisingly, the hustle creates a cycle where it feeds the ego, and the ego, in turn, then adds more fuel to the hustle.

Admiration and approval from others bolster self-esteem and strengthen ego/hustle's partnership.

The strongest egos often crave the most validation from others, which drives constant hustling and seeking out new achievement opportunities — *anything that ends in more praise.*

Unfortunately, ego also leads to some less appealing endings, one of many being *death by comparison.*

Ego is also known for the same kind of tricks the hustle pulls. At any given time, *you-know-who* can creep onto your shoulder, make an enormous chip, and then battle cry 'CRUSH THEM' before flitting off into the ether.

Have you questioned this inexplicable desire and an unstoppable drive to outperform (*nicely saying 'crush'*) your own friends, peers, and colleagues, at literally any opportunity, no matter the cost as it's happening? Try it.

Nothing is inherently wrong with accomplishments and validation and praise, make no mistake — affirmation and acknowledgment are essential. But are you getting the acknowledgment part in, too?

The mistake is in believing ego when it distorts and skews your reflection of self until everything you do is somehow reduced to how hyper-productive you can be.

A *'you are what you produce'* mentality forms. Then to avoid a drop in the outlandish results, you'll work harder and hustle more.

You get the next big feat done and suffer the drop in energy instead. *What else would you talk about if you didn't?*

Thus, the hustle also works to protect the ego and helps it grow up big and strong.

The imagined pressure and false urgency are highly stressful, even if fabricated, and incredibly damaging to you and to those around you.

If you're wondering,

> *'Oh yeah? What's the real damage — am I going to make too much money?'*

I've heard this all before, and seen the aftermath, which is never "too much money."

MINDSET

ΔΔΔ

Freeing up your head space will help calm and focus your attention on the task at hand.

The Brain Dump lets you know that work is here and now, for now.

That said, *it's time.*

The ANTI-Hustle BRAIN DUMP

1. Grab your handy dandy ANTI-Hustler's Companion Handbook at https://antihustlehandbook.com/toolbox
2. Flip to the Brain Dump Prompt for Chapter 7:
   Where are you struggling to have your team support you right now?
3. Put 10 minutes on the clock, and start writing!
4. Do the thing and once the timer dings, continue reading below with newfound clarity.

Hey, *look at you* — more clarity by the minute.

Or are you just relieved to have left the ego talk behind?

This was supposed to be about team management and energy preservation.

But is your ego mad tho?

I had to go there to get here: Making decisions that feed your ego instead of refilling your energy levels is a major threat to your business and overall success. Letting your ego take the wheel is one of the biggest risks you can take.

What the... How. Did. We. Get. Here.

CONSIDER THE HUSTLE-ISM:

" I CAN DO THIS FASTER MYSELF"

That's your ego talking. It's costing you time, finances, peace of mind, and oh so much more.

Here's the equation:

- If you say *"I can do this faster myself"* once a day, for a 30-minute task...

- And you work 5 days a week *(as if)*

- That hustle-ism *(your ego)* is costing you:

    - 2 ½ hours per week
    - 10 hours per month
    - 120 hours per year

That's FIVE whole days wasted. Literally a week of work. A week that could instead have been a much-needed vacation, but I know that's not what you're thinking...

So yes, it could have been a week of work that was far more productive if you simply dedicated time to developing a process and then delegating the task to a team member.

You already know that your energy is your most precious resource — you need it for far more than just Hulking out on every little task that comes your way.

That stuff is so much better outsourced or automated. Your business really needs YOU for legitimately the most important and the most urgent work — the BIG stuff.

> NOTE: *If you're struggling with identifying what's important vs urgent, check out Chapter 3.*

You also already know that Hustle Culture is built on the pretense that burnout is just "part of it" and nothing out of the ordinary for entrepreneurs.

Nothing to see here, keep hustling.

Now you know the hustle feeds your ego and your ego is more than happy to keep fueling the hustle. *Beware.*

What you might not know, exactly, is how all of those parts can intersect to impact your business in a powerful way and you really need to know how it all goes down.

Ego seeks validation and praise for always working too hard, sacrificing, and accomplishing everything independently, AKA the least efficient way possible.

How does this play out?

- Anything your entire team can do, you can somehow do better and faster. We all know because you've told us.

By taking on too much work, entrepreneurs may receive praise for their effort but at the cost of increased stress and potential burnout. If you don't yet care about those markers of success, it's also not cost-effective at all for many reasons.

If your team actually needs additional training and support and you're not just taking over for the ego grab later, keep in mind they very likely want to do the job correctly.

Many times an underperforming team can be resolved by assessing the situation and identifying

- skill gaps
- communication breakdowns
- misaligned expectations

Largely, 'just doing it better and faster' also prevents your team, to whom you pay real money, from actually doing their assigned and scheduled tasks so that you can gloat over the tasks yourself in trade for only praise.

- **This is a tough chapter for your ego, but honestly, someone is definitely not winning in this scenario.**

And to the reader who has no team yet, I want to clarify this is not a *'that's why I don't have a team'* moment, okay? This is an 'I have to figure out what's going on and work on fixing my systems' moment.

- **Your team is, well, they're your team, and they're all nice people so you'll just do the work — no worries.**

You know, if your team kinda sucks in the doing department, you don't have to skip to step 11 and fire them all today.

There are options: evaluate, run risk assessments, talk to your team together and one by one, implement job cards and performance assessments, and/or many other systems and processes that point to investing in your team and thus the business. I do not recommend investing in your ego instead.

- **You just like to be in touch with everyday operations.**

What are you even saying — do you even believe this?

Ego fuels the hustle and the desire to be seen as much as possible doing as much as possible. This leads entrepreneurs to take on more tasks than necessary, even when their team is totally capable of handling the workload. And worse, if your team is highly capable, chances are you're stifling their professional growth, and it's not even on your radar.

When you swoop in on tasks it prevents the team from taking responsibility and ever showcasing their abilities.

It's also 110% counterproductive.

You still have plenty of options to turn this around. And remember, counterproductive doesn't mean canceled…

Dust yourself off and try again.

∆∆∆

Start small. If you simply can not get your hands out of the pies, try a few simple things to start.

1. Celebrate when your team asks for help: If you want your team to ask for help so you can learn how to support them correctly and get the right systems in place, do this always.

You'll soon find that you have a more autonomous, trusting team who outperforms their old model and can tell you why.

2. Assume two things when you head into performance assessments or evaluations of any kind:

- This person has my best interests in mind
- This person is being totally honest with me

If you're screaming, that's too naive, or people will take advantage of you, or that is exactly how bad choices get made, etc., stop and ask yourself: if your goal is a productive conversation, why would you go into it any other way?

Let other people show you who they are. Don't make an ass of yourself by flexing your ego and chucking assumptions when you could simply exercise decency instead.

Effective risk management systems and other processes can be in place in your business and in your life to avoid common pitfalls that would otherwise impact you negatively.

∆∆∆

For simplicity's sake, you can also think about your next moves as a decision over how much impact you want and how to carefully exact that impact…

- **Let go and let ego** take the wheel, **OR**
- **Let go of ego** and take the wheel

Recognizing the interplay of ego, hustle culture, and energy preservation is crucial for entrepreneurs aiming to build, scale, and maintain successful businesses. Seeking validation and praise at the cost of increased stress and burnout is just an inefficient use of resources, even before considering the underutilization of a paid team.

Ego-driven decisions can also negatively impact the overall success and sustainability of a business since outcomes are often missing the critical metrics and the constructive communication that helps track to completion.

Your team is in the crossfire if you don't take back the wheel.

Meanwhile, entrepreneurs who build stronger and more effective teams and systems contribute to the success of their employees and ultimately the business. By addressing any actual underlying causes in tandem with ego, chances are you'll still get that feel-good praise, too.

The differences are also tangible when your business is optimized with multiple options for success versus when it was running on one kind of fuel alone: the unleaded blend of entrepreneurial energy, inconsolable ego, and brow sweat.

Common pitfalls are mitigated when your energy is spent in more balanced ways, and with a stronger foundation, it's easier to grow and scale your business. Remember, you can't fill anyone else's cup — your clients', your partner, your children, anyone's — if your cup is completely empty and your resources are unsustainable.

ACTION

△△△

Now it's time to take action and quiet the Hustle-isms and the occasional battle cry of your ego.

The tool of choice for Team Management & Energy Preservation is ... actually TWO TOOLS!

Remember, I reassured you this chapter was for you whether or not you had a team in place and I stand by that.

If you don't have a team in place, your tool for Chapter 7 is

THE ANTI-HUSTLER HANDBOOK
X
YOU ARE HERE

Your business was not destined to be a 1-man or woman show forever. Running a business solo can be exhausting. If you're still stuck in the Freelancer's Trap, you might not even have a backup to pick up the slack when you're all out of steam.

Trying to handle everything yourself can lead to burnout and less-than-ideal outcomes for your business.

Building a team will be essential to help you grow and scale your business.

Building a team also takes time. While you're still growing, there are tools and tactics available to help you get from where you are to where you want to go, without losing all your energy on the way.

I recommend working on identifying where and how you can optimize your business processes and strengthen your foundation, but the choices are yours.

Where you are right now, this minute in The ANTI-Hustler's Handbook is a fantastic place to be.

The Companion Handbook online will also provide you with additional tools and the workspace you need to practice.

By using the strategies and resources here in the book and online, you can build better systems and streamline processes that will help you simplify your workflow and preserve your energy. That way you can refocus your energy on strategic planning and growth.

When you're ready to scale and grow, the next resources will be right here ready and waiting to help you take your business to the next level.

∆∆∆

If you do have a team in place, your tool for Chapter 7 is

THE ERAM

In our coaching business, I coined the C.H.A.M.P model: *Caring, Helpful, Available, Motivating, Proactive*

Yes, we love it and it is motivational, but I'm telling you about it right now because I want you to know this...

> *I am normally really, really good with acronyms. I think CHAMP really seals the deal on you agreeing with me. It's not just CHAMP, though. First, it was CULTURE and now there are at least 3-5 more that just feel right.*

I have some really good acronym brainchildren out there that make me so proud. I mean, just beaming.

The ERAM is a *terrible* acronym. This is not one of those times.

A quick Google search of the term yields an acronym the Federal Aviation Administration uses for their computers: En Route Automation Modernization — yikes.

This is not the same as The ANTI-Hustle ERAM despite having the same terrible acronym name.

Zachary Wong, Ph.D., not the FAA, is responsible for the ERAM we'll be using. He wrote about it in his seminal book, *The Eight Essential People Skills for Project Management.*

I'm guessing Dr. Wong felt that REAM wasn't ideal messaging when trying to maximize team efficiency.

The good news? I did not come up with the ERAM acronym.

The better news? The ERAM will help you maximize your team, thus preserving your energy to focus on the right tasks.

∆∆∆

The acronym breaks down as follows:

- **E = Expectations:** Does your team member have absolute clarity on their job role, requirements, and success KPIs?

- **R = Resources:** Does your team member have all the necessary resources to ensure they can accomplish their job efficiently and effectively?

- **A = Ability:** Does your team member have the abilities required to succeed in their job role?

- **M = Motivation:** Does your team member have the appropriate motivation (both financial and fulfillment) to succeed in their job role?

Taking the baseline from Dr. Wong, I created an assessment and ensuing action steps all entrepreneurs can utilize to enhance team performance.

The ERAM works in a variety of different ways, all of which will benefit both you and your team collectively.

The ERAM can be…

- used for one specific team member, an entire department, or the entire team as a whole
- utilized for performance evaluations quarterly, bi-annually, annually, or as you deem necessary
- audited and reviewed by you (the business owner) or your management team

Find the following ERAM tools and more to start maximizing your team's performance by accessing the ANTI-Hustler's Companion Handbook at https://antihustlehandbook.com/toolbox

EXPECTATIONS

- My #1 job role is…
- Other job requirements are…
- Detail-oriented…
- Willingness to express when there can be improvements on processes

RESOURCES

- I'm provided a detailed SOP…
- I have video training
- I utilize the following tools…
- I'd like to have the following resources…

ABILITY

- I'm very confident in executing…
- I'm fairly confident in executing…
- I could use help in executing…
- I don't feel ___ is within my ability
- I feel my ___ ability is not being utilized

MOTIVATION

- I work with company because…
- I want to make $X
- I want to work *insert hours*
- My personal goal(s) are…
- The *company can help me* facilitate my goals by…

Up next: How to execute the ERAM, the *ANTI-Hustle way*.

1. Team member fills out ERAM template

When you share the ERAM template with your team, make sure they understand the purpose behind the tool first.

The ERAM is all about maximizing performance through *clarification* and *optimization*.

> Earlier during the Self-Assessment portion of the book, remember the part about the latent anxiety and resistance that typically exists with test-taking, regardless of explanation or pretense?
>
> For the ERAM to work best, you have to make sure your team knows this isn't a test to judge them.

The purpose is not to put team members on the chopping block or even to make them feel that way.

2. Review responses for RED/GREEN flags

Reviewing the ERAM is private and should only be completed by either you or the manager of the team member audited. Do NOT review ERAM templates live with team members. The goal of the review is to spot both **RED (concerning)** and **GREEN (positive)** flags.

A few prompts to consider:

- Are we on the same page in terms of job responsibilities and expectations?
- Are we providing the appropriate resources for this team member?
- Are we maximizing the right abilities of this team member?
- Are we as a company able to facilitate the goals of this team member?

Keep in mind the list above is not comprehensive. Feel free to add more! Remember, *options*.

3. Prep for/schedule a 1-on-1 review with team member

Here's what I recommend you compile prior to the call:

- Remind them of the purpose of this tool. TO MAXIMIZE!
- Share at least 3 things you are happy with in regards to their ERAM and overall performance
- Share at least 3 things you either want to improve or at least get clarification on based on their ERAM
- Is there anything you'd like to add to their responsibility list? Do they want to do those tasks?

4. Get feedback from team member by asking questions...

- How did they feel going through the ERAM?
- How do they feel about their performance recently?
- Do they feel aligned with the direction of the company?
- Do they want to continue working with the company?
- Is there anything the company can do to improve the experience of the team member?
- Is there anything the team member believes they should be doing differently in order to maximize results?

5. Create an action plan and set a review date

The action plan comes down to one prompt: **What specific KPIs will be tracked to measure success?** Is it a sales metric? Client retention data? Or perhaps how much time they are saving you in particular?

Ideally, the review date should be set for 90 days later. The team member wouldn't do another ERAM then but instead review the previous ERAM together to identify any gaps and gains.

The tool has a cumulative, compounding effect over time.

- Your team becomes more proficient in their roles.
- You preserve more of your critically valuable energy.
- Your team becomes better managed and organized.
- You reap the rewards of team maximization.
- And it only gets better as the months and years pass.
- This is the ANTI-ego method of team management.

Look at you, ANTI-Hustling like a leader.

TOOLS & RESOURCES

△△△

Access ALL the resources in this chapter and more at:
https://antihustlehandbook.com/toolbox

1. **Hiring Resources:** There's a slew of recommendations in the ANTI-Hustler's Companion Handbook, but here are a few personal favorites: FreeUp, RepStack, Level9 Virtual, Upwork, and Onlinejobs.ph

2. **Enneagram:** A personality test to better understand how you and your team members both operate.

3. **Job Scorecard & Hiring Templates:** Clearly defined roles, responsibilities, and KPIs help your team succeed.

THE CLOSER
THE REFRAMING TECHNIQUE

△△△

Before you go, really reflect on the progress you've made over the course of just this chapter.

Revisit the negative statements from the start of Team Management & Energy Preservation.

Right now is the perfect time to silence the noise and strengthen the signal by trading out the Hustle-isms for empowering statements to help you shift your mindset and strengthen your commitment to a more balanced and intentional life.

	TEAM MANAGEMENT & ENERGY PRESERVATION: REFRAME	
	From Hustle-ism... *Why am I so stressed all the time?*	**To ANTI-Hustle-ism...** *I'm in my flow state, my comfort zone*
1.	"My team is not pulling their weight. I'm doing too much!"	
2.	"I can do this faster myself."	
3.	"Only I can do [insert task] correctly."	
4.	"Hiring someone will take too long."	
5.	"If I automate, the tech will break or something will get lost in the mix — I just know it."	

NEXT STEPS

You just ANTI-Hustled your way through Chapter 7!

△△△

REMEMBER

Return to the **Self Assessment**, again and again, to reassess your growth on the ANTI-Hustle journey

Each time, record the date, individual segment scores, and the **Total Balance Factor** to map your progress

ONWARD

1. Go back and check your scores on **Self-Assessment**

2. Identify which segment & chapter you prioritized up next

3. Head there and dig in where it matters most, ANTI-Hustler

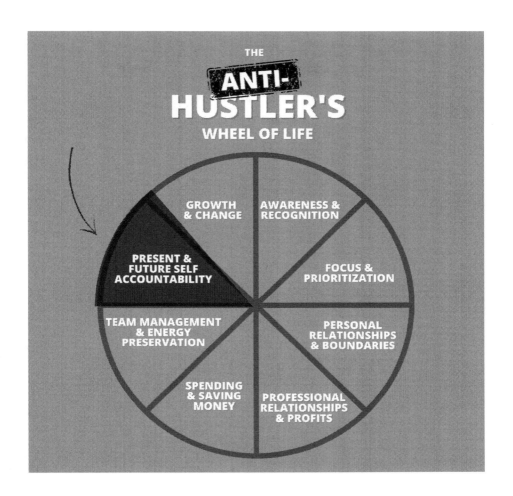

— CHAPTER 08 —

PRESENT & FUTURE SELF-ACCOUNTABILITY

FOUNDATION

△△△

Staying motivated and on track can be super challenging.

Luckily, there are ways to make sure you stay accountable to yourself and reach your goals, but no one said discipline was easy, either.

To have a breakthrough with this chapter, a mindset shift is necessary.

From now on, you have to reconcile that you'll need to stay accountable to two versions of yourself:

1. Your Present Self AND
2. Your Future Self

Remember, *true success* — as defined in this handbook — is when your Present Self is able to enjoy the opportunities you have now while setting your Future Self up for more choices that will increase your happiness in the future.

If you find yourself constantly over-booking your calendar or agreeing to meetings outside of reasonable work hours, it's likely your Present Self is sabotaging your Future Self *(and also you're low-key miserable)*.

I've been there many times, and it typically sounds like this:

Present Self:
"Absolutely I can get that project done in the next 5 days"

FAST FORWARD to 5 days later and feeling disheartened. I'm still working at 11 pm (or 3 am) to get the project finished and it's somehow still surprising and disappointing when it happens… even though it always happens.

Future Self:
"Why do I constantly punish myself like this? This is so stupid"

It sounds familiar, right? It's *still* surprising, right?

There is *definitely* a better way…

∆∆∆

The goal of every chapter is to provide you with actionable steps to beat the hustle and keep ANTI-Hustling your way to greater success.

To do that, you'll have to quiet the noisy Hustle-isms and redefine success.

The sound of the grating, choice-hating indignance has probably drowned out more good ideas than you'd like to count and cost more than a few zzz's.

Do a quick review of what got you here so you can figure out how to ANTI-Hustle your way right out the door.

PRESENT & FUTURE SELF-ACCOUNTABILITY

- *"My actual life right now and where I thought I'd be at this point in my life are very, very different"*
- *"Life isn't the greatest at this exact moment, but that's all going to change when ___ happens"*
- *"What?! No. My dream life is nothing like my life now"*
- *"You have to hustle to win - you're playing a dangerous game by telling people this BS"*
- *"Pretend all you want, but it IS a competition — EVERYTHING is: There will always be judges, winners, and losers"*

When people hear accountability, the responses are a pretty mixed bag. It's not uncommon to hear some groans and a lot of chair shifting.

Panickers will panic, and the resident complainer says what everyone's thinking, *"You serious, Clark?"*

It doesn't have to be that way.

Before this gets out of hand, learning what accountability **ISN'T** will help you cross some of the inhibitions off your list.

~~Punishment~~ ANTI-HUSTLED

One of the most common misconceptions about accountability is equating it with punishment. In reality, accountability is about taking responsibility and being answerable for the results of those actions.

Simply put, every action has an equal or opposite reaction. There will always be consequences — that's science! But consequences are not the essence of accountability.

~~Blaming with paperwork~~ ANTI-HUSTLED

Blame is about assigning fault, while accountability is about taking responsibility. Blame focuses on the past, while accountability focuses on the future and finding solutions.

This is a big one — huge differences that are easy to see without your readers.

Strong recommendation: use the past to inform your decisions and leave it there.

You can't live there, you can't work there, you can't change anything there.

Why creep around and loom in the past? Stay forward facing.

~~Only for corporate bosses~~ ANTI-HUSTLED

There are so many different measures of accountability. I'm sure there are some only for corporate bosses — something like Scrooge McDuck's 270 KPIs to accountability.

Who knows?

Everyone should use their own individual goals and information to create an accountability plan that works for now and later.

There is plenty of work to be done with accountability, PROPER.

The essential framework for accountability is based on creating a culture of trust, collaboration, and continuous improvement.

~~A one-time thing~~ ANTI-HUSTLED

This is not a "just push through" kind of deal. Some people think accountability is a one-time event because the only accountability they've ever experienced was poorly implemented in the past.

With full confidence, accountability will be an ongoing process to get the results you want. Continually evaluating your actions, learning from mistakes, and making necessary changes to improve outcomes are part of the setup.

~~Micromanaging to the nth degree~~ ANTI-HUSTLED

Finally your micromanaging has gone so far that now you've finally started micromanaging yourself. LOL — no, that's not what this is. And I don't want to "Well actually," but micromanagement can actually hinder accountability by discouraging autonomy and innovation.

Accountability is about creating a supportive environment that encourages people to take ownership of their work and make decisions based on shared goals and values. Boom!

~~Hustle culture perfection~~ ANTI-HUSTLED

Hustle culture says to do "it" until you get it right and then do "it" over and over and over until it's perfect. I'm thinking of Black Swan right now and feeling nauseous — also not what this is, very thankfully.

Accountability doesn't mean being perfect or even striving for perfection. I let that go a long time ago. Being honest about mistakes, taking responsibility, and learning from failure improves future outcomes.

MINDSET

△△△

Freeing up your head space will help calm and focus your attention on the task at hand.

The Brain Dump lets you know that work is here and now, for now.

That said, *it's time.*

The ANTI-Hustle BRAIN DUMP

1. Grab your handy dandy ANTI-Hustler's Companion Handbook at https://antihustlehandbook.com/toolbox

2. Flip to the Brain Dump Prompt for Chapter 8: **Where in your life are you leaning into blaming versus taking accountability?**

3. Put 10 minutes on the clock, and start writing!

4. Do the thing and once the timer dings, continue reading below with newfound clarity.

Hey, *look at you* — more clarity by the minute.

It's time to start by clearing the air on accountability. You know what it's not.

How about what it **IS**? To be accountable is to take responsibility for your actions and commitments.

To whom? It's about being answerable to someone, and you just signed up for Present and Future You.

For what? Reaching goals, meeting deadlines, and making progress, creating a culture of care.

In a nutshell, accountability is the glue that helps turn your plans into reality.

Easy enough — except it's not.

Accountability happens to be one of the toughest things to get right, to track, to talk about, to do, and to implement pretty much ever.

If you listen carefully, you can even hear the challenges behind the Hustle-isms that got you here... I'm still expecting that you generate your own reframed Hustle-isms at the back of the chapter.

So what's the hiccup? Why the pushback on accountability?

Resistance to change: Accountability often involves stepping away from how we got to where we are in order to get where we need to go. Embracing change can be scary and uncomfortable, making it hard to fully commit to being accountable. *(See CH. 9)*

> **Try Instead ->** Failure isn't a dirty word. But it IS an opportunity to grow.

Fear of failure: Saying the F-word yet [failure]? Plenty of people avoid being held accountable because it requires admitting that goals or expectations weren't met. It's tough to face disappointment, both in ourselves and from others.

> **Try Instead ->** Accountability helps to define the help and support you need to better meet your goals on time and in full. [Honestly, this one is what turned accountability around for me.]

Lack of motivation: Staying accountable requires a consistent level of motivation. *Ugh - who has that?* It's not always easy to maintain that motivation, especially when we're faced with obstacles or setbacks. Also, life, right?

> **Try Instead ->** Motivation doesn't mean jumping up and down, but it does mean being committed to getting the job done. *[This shift is MONUMENTAL. Motivation isn't Jazzercise energy 24/7.]*

Procrastination: If you find it hard to hold yourself accountable, putting things off or struggling with time management is super common. Procrastination can make it challenging to stay on top of our commitments, but it's also something totally figure-out-able. *(See CH. 3)*

> **Try Instead ->** Why am I avoiding this? What do I need that I don't have to be successful? How can I get it? Who can help me do that? *[Goes with my other favorite — Topic: Support, Care: High]*

Ambiguity in goals: If goals are not specific, clear, and measurable… do I need to finish? (I do because this is a choose-your-own-adventure book.) Success is difficult - if not unattainable - when you don't know what you're doing and the finish line is unclear. It is easier to stay accountable when there are well-defined objectives. Every. Time.

> **Try Instead ->** Clarification isn't just extra work. Clearly defining your goals also creates a plan and a timeline that reduces work.

ACTION

△△△

It's time to take action to quiet the Hustle-isms, but this isn't just any action…

How do you enact accountability for both Present You and Future You to still enjoy now but also ensure happiness later?

Tall order! Is it impossible? Everything is impossible until you define it, design it, and do it.

Then it's not impossible anymore — *it's done.* The tool for Chapter 8 is …

The ANTI-Hustle Define, Design, Do

STEP 1: Define

The critical first step is defining an end goal.

Without one, you'll aimlessly walk, run, or climb through a sea of never-ending obstacles only to reach an indefinite destination without true happiness or fulfillment.

Yikes, right?

Without a finish line, you not only guarantee burnout but ensure you stay oppressed by hustle culture. I hope you won't willingly choose that route when you now know. Especially when you have so many other better options.

In order to have accountability to your Present and Future self, there must be clarity on the end goal.

Let's back up: To be sure, you do have clarity on the problem.

You're doing too much.

You're drowning.

You're overwhelmed.

You're a failure.

But you do not have any idea and even less clarity on why you hustled yourself into a corner. Now you feel trapped.

Remember Mo Farah and Usain Bolt?

They're unparalleled winners. Literally, they are winners that are not parallel with one another. Their finish lines are different.

The lesson here is that by defining the finish line, the goal, and your own success, the likelihood of you achieving it is exponentially higher.

Unparalleled winners. Non-competitors.

This will take work. It won't just come naturally to everyone.

Many people don't know what they want in life - or what will make them happy - because they're so indoctrinated into the hustle culture of simply doing more.

In my experience, most people haven't created their personal version of success for 2 primary reasons:

1. "I don't know what will make me happy and fulfilled"
2. "Even if I did, I don't think I'd ever hit those goals"

Borrow My Notes...

So what if you don't know right now? Define it anyway!

You have the right to happiness and success. You can't have it without first defining it. They ARE mutually exclusive.

So you're unsure of what it may be right now? That's okay!

It's okay because you can stop right now and take action.

But, a tool within a tool?!? When it's time, it's time...

The ANTI-Hustle BRAIN DUMP

1. Consider the Brain Dump Prompt here: **Brain dump all the things that make you happy.**

   You could also identify a series of accomplishments that you believe could potentially provide you with satisfaction, fulfillment, and happiness.

   If you achieve what you listed out, but you're still not happy, come back to this journal, and optimize.

   Happiness & success will emerge from optimization!
2. Put 10 minutes on the clock, and start writing!
3. Do the thing and once the timer dings, continue reading below with newfound clarity.

As for the fear of failure, ever heard the one about "shooting for the stars, and landing on the moon"?

You may think you want a Bugatti and a $10 Million home with a private island *(the stars)*.

But when you get a spacious east-side home and a Jeep Wrangler, it could be the happiest you've ever been (moon).

Hustle culture and the fear of failure are strange bedfellows.

Hustle culture says to do more and more and more and never stop while snuggled up to fear of failure, which says do not ever do because you might fail more often than not.

What a scam. Don't allow fear of failure to stop you from trying to achieve what you believe will make you happy. *(See CH. 9)*

If you can still surprise yourself when you know the outcome — hello working all night and all day — then surely you can surprise yourself by suddenly realizing you're midway to your goal, *happy as a clam*, having ANTI-Hustled your way there.

Short-term sacrifices are required for long-term goals, but there's no purpose in sacrificing for the sake of it.

If your plan includes an option for the sacrifice, be sure it's necessary. Make it worthwhile and purposeful and make sure it truly is only as necessary.

While working on the *Define* section of this journal, it is PARAMOUNT to set realistic and achievable goals with an end in sight. You must.

The key to self-accountability is not just setting realistic and time-bound goals, but goals with purpose.

Without a clear purpose, entrepreneurs have proven time and again they will underperform or overshoot or miss the mark entirely.

So, ask yourself:

- What will I do with this additional income I'm working so hard to acquire?

- What will I do with this newfound time freedom I'm working so hard to acquire?

The clearer the vision, the easier it is to stay accountable to the plan.

In the next stage, Design, you'll map out the steps you need to take to reach your goal. The steps are an easy way to chunk your tasks into smaller pieces to make success measurable and time-sensitive.

Have you heard the one about the best way to eat an elephant?
— One bite at a time.

STEP 2: Design

With these goals clearly defined, the newfound clarity alone should feel as if a literal weight has been lifted from your shoulders. The monkey is thrown from your back so to speak.

No longer are you just working more for the sake of working.

You're working for something specific and important to you.

Hot damn! You are ANTI-hustling! There's more ahead.

The next step? Designing the path.

Self-Accountability really kicks into high gear at this point.

Present Self will also have to sacrifice for your Future Self to live the life you want. This has to be planned very carefully.

Consider the treasure map below. Note: You can find the *ANTI-Hustle Treasure Map in the Companion Handbook*.

What key destinations (milestones) are on the path to your ultimate goal? To effectively implement the *Define, Design, Do* planning journal, have no more than 5-ish key milestones along the path to your success.

A 20-step plan for your ultimate goal(s) is likely overkill. Chill.

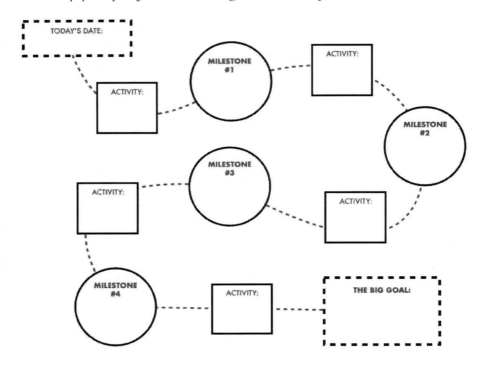

For example, your ultimate goal is to no longer work on Fridays within the next 6 months. Consider this hypothetical designed roadmap:

Ultimate Goal: Take Fridays Off

- Milestone #1: Reschedule Recurring Friday Meetings (Complete Within 45 Days)

- Milestone #2: Create SOPs To Delegate Client Mgmt (Complete Within 90 Days)

- Milestone #3: Hire Client Success Manager (Complete Within 120 Days)

- Milestone #4: 2 Months of CSM Shadow Before Takeover (Complete Within 6 Months)

Ultimate Goal: Take Fridays Off (Complete Within 6 Months)

Borrow My Notes...

Take this opportunity to reset. Remove any restrictions already building up in your mind right now. You know who you are...

> *"But what if I'm not 100% certain what milestones I have to hit in order to accomplish my goal?"* or *"But I have 5 different goals I'm working towards."*

That's okay.

Moving forward, let's get it out of the way since we're resetting. Expect to fail. It's unlikely on your first go-round you'll nail exactly what you want and the perfect milestones or timeline to hit it.

Right on track!

Revision is an expected, necessary part of the process also known as optimization — make it work for you.

Remember, this is what self-accountability is for. When you slip up on your path, you have a system and process to audit and change course.

When looking at the milestones above, it's totally normal to have come up with 3-5 completely different milestones to achieve the "Take Fridays Off" goal. Options!

In time, you'll lord over the dominion of design with expert maneuvering and planning, but for now... only having an idea of what the milestones should be is absolutely okay!

You can optimize along the way when you know more from experience too.

Having 2, 5, or 7 journals going at once is fine.

So long as you feel they are purposeful, not superfluous, and you're not hustling to achieve them because society says so.

Lastly, the 'end goal' is never really the end of the process, right? You're very unlikely to hit all in a series of goals and think:

> **"Welp, that'll do it. I've accomplished everything I've ever wanted"** (I'm not salivating at how cool that would be. Are you? Of course not, who does that?)

When the inevitable "next goal" arises, you'll have a journal to hold yourself accountable. And to optimize.

STEP 3: Do

This third step of the journal process is the most self-explanatory, but also it's the lynchpin of all three steps.

Meaning if step 3 doesn't happen, nothing actually happens.

And you probably don't need to hear this, but just in case you do: ***Nothing can be accomplished without the work.***

Considering you picked up The ANTI-Hustler's Handbook, I'm guessing you've already been "do"-ing plenty of work but without purpose or direction.

With the two prerequisite steps laid out, your actions have a purpose. Now it's all about staying accountable to your Present & Future Self doing the big work, hitting milestones, and achieving goals.

TOOLS & RESOURCES

ΔΔΔ

Access ALL the resources in this chapter and more at:
https://antihustlehandbook.com/toolbox

1. **Spoils Of ~~War~~ Work:** What exactly are you going to do with your business "winnings"?

2. **Treasure Map:** Consider this as your personal "Yellow Brick Road." What's the goal we're working towards, and the activities and milestones needed to achieve it?

3. **Success Calculator:** How much money is enough money? This calculator will give you the financial clarity you need to live your dream life (See CH. 6)

THE CLOSER
THE REFRAMING TECHNIQUE

△△△

Before you go, really reflect on the progress you've made over the course of just this chapter. Revisit the Hustle-isms from Present & Future Self Accountability. Now is the perfect time to silence the noise and strengthen the signal.

Reframe the -isms and trade them out for empowering statements to help you shift your mindset and strengthen your commitment to a more balanced and intentional life.

	PRESENT & FUTURE SELF ACCOUNTABILITY: REFRAME	
	From Hustle-ism... *Why am I so stressed all the time?*	**To ANTI-Hustle-ism...** *I'm in my flow state, my comfort zone*
1.	"My actual life right now and where I thought I'd be at this point in my life are very, very different."	
2.	"Life isn't the greatest at this exact moment, but that's all going to change when ___ happens."	
3.	"What?! No. My dream life is nothing like my life right now."	
4.	"You have to hustle to win — you're playing a dangerous game by telling people this BS."	
5.	"Pretend all you want, but it IS a competition — EVERYTHING is — there will always be judges, winners, and losers."	

NEXT STEPS

You just ANTI-Hustled your way through Chapter 8!

△△△

REMEMBER

Return to the **Self Assessment**, again and again, to reassess your growth on the ANTI-Hustle journey

Each time, record the date, individual segment scores, and the **Total Balance Factor** to map your progress

ONWARD

1. Go back and check your scores on **Self-Assessment**

2. Identify which segment & chapter you prioritized up next

3. Head there and dig in where it matters most, ANTI-Hustler

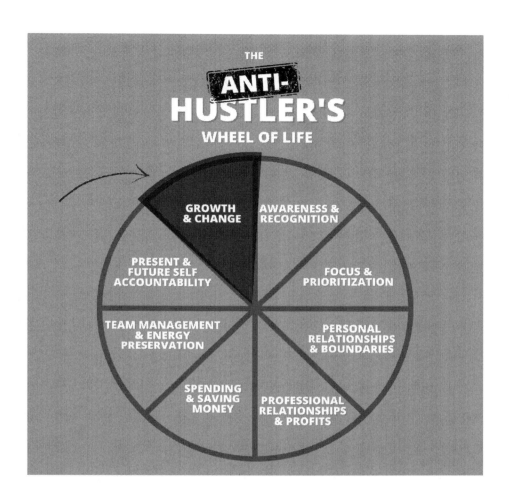

— CHAPTER 09 —

GROWTH & CHANGE

FOUNDATION

△△△

Growth and change are inevitable.

I refrained from diving deep into the hourglass metaphor in the first part of the book, but you deserve a little more insight here.

Everyone has their own hourglass...

And everyone is born with a terminal death diagnosis.

What I mean is, no time is truly promised.

To really be successful, honestly successful, you must embrace growth and change as it happens. You can't keep borrowing sand from a Future You that might not ever be.

Don't WTF me so fast, I'm honestly not being dark or morbid.

I only want you to understand the weight of the implications of saving up all the happiness, growth, and change for your Future Self.

It's... well, it's not good.

Why not?

In order to succeed, it is essential to experience growth and change. It can be uncomfortable. Okay, it can be very uncomfortable — fine, incredibly uncomfortable. But, necessary.

Growth allows us to develop new skills and knowledge. Change challenges us to think creatively and find new ways of doing things. Without these two things, we would become stagnant, and our business, among other things, would soon stand still.

Remember, hustle culture strives for monotony: work harder, do more, and more, then some more, and how about some more?

There is no growth and change in monotony — *it is the flatline.*

ΔΔΔ

The goal of every chapter is to provide you with actionable steps to beat the hustle and keep ANTI-Hustling your way to greater success. To do that, you'll have to quiet the noisy Hustle-isms and redefine success.

A friend once told me the key to genuine happiness is "the overcoming of known obstacles."

Having clarity on the problem is the first step to solving it.

GROWTH & CHANGE

- "Look, it's just not gonna happen. I tried the best I could, and it is what it is"

- "Ugh! I shouldn't have listened to anyone else - this happens every single time"

- "I'm on the hot mess express, struggle-bussin' my way to the end of the day"

- "Failure isn't an option. I'll figure it out on my own - I have to. I put a lot of money and time into this"

- "I should already be there by now "

∆∆∆

Didn't you come here for opportunity? Entrepreneurship is all about taking risks and pushing boundaries.

I always say *how essential it is to be comfortable with 'no'* in business, but that doesn't come easy.

Just like you need to be comfortable with change and growth, it doesn't come easy at first.

There's a ridiculous amount of *uncomfortable* until you get to the *comfortable*. Then, you get to your comfort zone. Think about it like a new couch, you have to break it in a little, right?

All the businesses around you are growing and changing too. Why? Clients and market trends are always shifting, and entrepreneurs are known for being adaptable.

Do you know what supports growth and change? I'm gonna say it again… smart systems and a good team in place.

Safety nets are there to make progress and take smart risks.

These setups are available so you can use what got you here, your brain, and all your brainchildren to the best of your ability.

The world needs you to do that.

You growing and changing and experimenting and trying new things is crucial to find what works best for the rest of us *(oh, and your business too)*.

To do that, are you willing to consider that you're open to failure? *Or is it still too soon?*

Failure will remain an inevitable part of the entrepreneurial journey. It's how you recover from failure that really matters.

Fall down 7 times, get up 8 — *Forget math, it's motivational!*

Still can't say it? Too ingrained? How about some *failure* affirmations to practice on your way to the comfort zone?

- Failure is tough to swallow, especially when I've invested so much time and effort into this project. The key is to maintain perspective.
- Failure is not the end of the world, even if I feel like it is right this second. It's just an opportunity to try again and do better next time.
- Failure isn't permanent. I win, or I learn. There's no loss in lessons learned and insight gained. Next!

No matter how you say it, it's all about accepting what things you can't change and focusing on what you can control.

In other words, don't waste time and energy dwelling on past mistakes or setbacks, even if they're big flopping failures.

Assess. Strengthen. Optimize. Change.

Combine that with a sense of humor, open disposition, and perspective — perhaps then, the end truly is not nigh.

Try again.

MINDSET

∆∆∆

Freeing up your head space will help calm and focus your attention on the task at hand.

The Brain Dump lets you know that work is here and now, for now.

That said, *it's time.*

The ANTI-Hustle BRAIN DUMP

1. Grab your handy dandy ANTI-Hustler's Companion Handbook at https://antihustlehandbook.com/toolbox
2. Flip to the Brain Dump Prompt for Chapter 9: **Where is fear of failure stunting your growth?**
3. Put 10 minutes on the clock, and start writing!
4. Do the thing and once the timer dings, continue reading below with newfound clarity.

Hey, *look at you* — more clarity by the minute.

Learning that you have to quiet the Hustle-isms is foundational.

But what about learning HOW to quiet the Hustle-isms?

Remember, Hustle-isms won't just come in the form of self-talk.

The hustle is very multi-faceted.

Here's the thing: The FEAR of failure is far greater than failure itself in most cases.

The fear of failure often leads to poor decision-making, or worse, indecision.

See, if you make a *bad decision* - which inherently can only be in retrospect. Nobody purposely makes a bad decision from the onset - you try that handy dandy 4-step framework I shared earlier.

Remember? Assess. Strengthen. Optimize. Change.

No biggie! The failure you were so worried about turned out to not be such a big deal after all.

Seneca, the famous stoic, posited: "We suffer more in imagination than in reality."

Well if that ain't THE definition of fear of failure, I don't know what is.

Okay, back to indecision.

When you are so worried about a misstep, a bad decision, or a potential failure, you can become paralyzed.

Your mind plays the failure reels in your head over and over. It warns you of all the catastrophic things that will happen with this failure.

So you do nothing. In the absence of action sits indecision.

And indecision is far worse than no decision.

Indecision guarantees at least stagnation, and at worst, you regress.

The difference between regression and failure is there is no 4-step framework available.

What is there to assess? You did nothing.

There's no optimizations to be had, because you never tried in the first place.

You've heard the cliche: "You gotta risk it for the biscuit", right?

This is what it means to have skin in the game. You can't win unless you *play* in the game.

Sitting on the sidelines guarantees you have no shot.

You want to hit home runs? You need to be willing to strike out, and sometimes strike out BIG - Like striking out in the bottom of the 9th in the World Series *big*.

The good news? Usually the strikeouts aren't as big as you thought they'd be. *Don't you know there's 162 games in an MLB season? At least 70% of those strikeouts won't matter.*

∆∆∆

So often, I hear conversations about failure. Rather than pitting hustle culture as an adversary, *and a formidable one*, people are quick to counter failure instead.

When people say *failure is **not** an option*, I rarely have the heart to correct them. But maybe I should more often.

Honestly, failure is **ALWAYS** an option.

In fact, failure is the most readily available and easily accessible option in all scenarios.

Quitting is *always* on the table. There's ramifications to that *failure*, sure, but it's most definitely an option.

But the thing is — failure isn't terminal. I mean, in most cases. I can make that kind of joke, I had open heart surgery. *(Haven't read PART I: The Hustle? Maybe today is the day).*

I'm just saying failure doesn't HAVE TO be negative every single time. As such, there are some other options maybe you haven't considered.

Failure gets a really bad rap on these mean streets of entrepreneurship as being solely negative.

Okay, naysayer in aisle 3 - I hear you, it can also be negative. You *can* also drown in an inch of water.

So, for the context of this book, if you tack on resilience and refined systems and put a good team in place, failure doesn't have to mean that everything is falling apart.

Instead, failure is more than likely a prerequisite. For what, you query?

If you have a pile of hopes and dreams and you're the kind of person who pulls every loose thread with passion — and most entrepreneurs do — failure is in your future… *if you don't already know it very well.*

Whatever you hope to achieve in your personal and professional life, there's a very strong likelihood of a mountain of obstacles and failures arising before you as you choose the right path(s).

It's through growth in the act of optimization and continuing effort you will eventually succeed.

Save this for later…

The ANTI-Hustle Pocket Proffer

> *"Be willing to hear no, more than they are willing to say it."*
> — Alex Schlinsky

Heck yes I just quoted myself – It's my book!

ACTION

△△△

Start taking action right now by reimagining failure as something else — it's a pretty easy reframe.

Remember the different values for **36%?** Even when it's an F, you can think about failure as an opportunity for growth and change, rather than just a big fat F.

The tool specifically for **Growth & Change**?

The ANTI-Hustle Fear Setting

A Tim Ferris special!

It's only appropriate to have a Tim Ferris tool in the ANTI-Hustler's Handbook.

The *4-Hour Workweek* was one of my initial inspirations to focus more on *lifestyle design* as opposed to hustle culture.

AND, another of his books, *Tools of Titans*, was the inspiration for writing a non-linear book focused on actionable support and tools.

Thanks, Tim.

Let's start with a particular scenario. Feel with me, if you will…

Scrolling through Instagram, past the photos of a college friend roaming Paris, past the ads for the local gym that just opened.

Past the gallery post on the "5 effective ways to use AI for your business," And almost scrolling past a screenshot of a Stripe account — *Almost.*

Just gonna slide that scroll back up to see what's happening,

The poster isn't a close personal friend... they aren't even an acquaintance. It's some E-commerce guru you've been following for god knows how long or why,

I'm just as curious as the next person, okay? Tired of listening, volume down, and the post reads like this:

Just passed $100k in revenue this month, and it's not even the 10th yet! So proud of this accomplishment, and can't wait to break more records! #Grinding #Ecom #KeepHustling #DontStop #CantStop #Money #Dreams

Your thumb isn't even on the screen anymore. Posts like this always make you feel some type of way...

Is this the mix of emotions?

- *Skepticism?*
- *Inspiration?*
- *Jealousy?*
- *Frustration?*
- *Irritation?*
- *Disappointment?*

Thoughts dart through your mind at light speed:

- *"How is he doing this - this guy?"*
- *"This is bullshit, right? It's Photoshop right?"*
- *"Why am I struggling to make $100k in a whole year let alone 10 days?"*

Worse ... Head shaking,

"I don't know how he does it."

It's better just to close the app now and put your phone away.

Deep breath in. "I expand with abundance." Deep breath out.

△△△

If you're here reading this, hi — there's a lot of truth up there, huh?

First, before anything else, you likely are enjoying more abundance than the next person. No one is comparing — you made a choice that some people never will which means you have a little more in your abundance basket.

Second, what is this that we do? Why do entrepreneurs have this collective experience? Why do we...

- Care about the money other people make at all?
- Kick ourselves in 3 seconds over a Stripe screenshot?
- Devalue our work over photoshopped screenshots?
- Make decisions about our worth with 0 context?

This is a phenomenon. A truly shared experience.

To turn this thing on its head. You have to work through a reframing process.

It's already been established that abundance exists in your life and is substantial — try anchoring yourself to that idea to reground yourself.

Then, instead of reacting in shame from feelings of failure and negative self-worth, first, try and decide what is actually true. Of the situation, what is definitely true?

The sure-fire facts about this financial comparison phenomenon. What do you know for fact here?

Nothing.

You don't know …

- What is legitimate or what isn't
- What actual profits are being made
- What the exact circumstances are

So you do know *something*. What you do know for sure is…

You had 0 control over the alleged financial victory.

Real or fake, it doesn't have anything to do with you.

> I hear you out there: **BUT WHAT IF IT IS REAL AND I AM THE LEAST MONEY MAKING ENTREPRENEUR IN THE WHOLE-WIDE WORLD?**
>
> You can't be that because everyone else here thinks they're that, resulting in an even tie for 1st and last place.
>
> **It's just that way sometimes.**

Strong opinions regarding comparison and specifically the financial comparison phenomenon:

- Comparison is the thief of joy
- If you're interested in achievement, that makes sense
- If you're interested in it but can't be happy for another person's achievement, why bother to focus on it?
- These posts rarely motivate anyone in a healthy way
- Social media is one big highlight reel, not real life

△△△

So, what does *Fear Setting* have to do with this?

We are so often told to "define our goals" (Heck, in this book alone, I sound like a World Cup compilation), but we are so rarely recommended to "define our fears."

That's exactly what Fear Setting is all about.

Remember that Seneca line earlier? The one about suffering more in imagination than in reality? *Yea, that one!*

What if you had a tool to brain dump all the potential worst case scenarios of a looming decision?

And then a method to review potential ways to avoid those worst case scenarios from happening?

And even further, if they did happen, what actions would you take to recover from those worst case scenarios?

Is it possible you'd realize the worst case scenarios aren't as bad as your mind made you believe?

That's Fear Setting in a nutshell.

A tool to allay your fears by removing your pesky emotions from the driver's seat and firmly planting pragmatism in its wake.

And if you go through the tool and realize the worst case scenarios are far too risky to *make the play*, then don't!

Here's how it works in action... You can grab the template in the Companion Handbook at https://antihustlehandbook.com/toolbox

GROWTH & CHANGE | 303

STEP 1:
What's the decision in question that stimulates your FEAR?

- The prompt is "What if I X"?, but this is your Fear Setting journal, feel free to make it any prompt you see fit. Options!
- It could be a personal or professional decision. There is no prompt too big or too small
- Some examples follow…
    - *What if I take a 1-month vacation?*
    - *What if I make a $10,000 mentorship investment?*
    - *What if I dump my girlfriend?*
    - *What if I fire my Client Success Manager?*

STEP 2: Define

- On the far left column, list out all the potential worst-case scenarios you can imagine stemming from this decision
- Go wild here. What's the worst that can happen?
- For Example: If I take a 1-month vacation I could lose all of my clients, OR If I dump my girlfriend, I'll lose all of our mutual friends

STEP 3: Prevent

- How could you prevent these potential worst-case scenarios from happening?
- If you tinker with the *input*, could it potentially affect the output?
- For Example: *If I tell my clients in advance that I'm vacationing and assure them our Client Success Manager will be there to support them, they'll be much more understanding*

STEP 4: Repair

- Let's say the worst case scenario unfortunately plays out. Breathe. How can we fix it and optimize it to move forward?

- For example, *We lost 5 clients while I was on vacation. I can A) Call each of them to see if I can reactivate their accounts by alleviating their concerns or offering a discount. B) I can begin a new client acquisition campaign to recoup lost clients and revenues.*

Survey the landscape of Define, Prevent, and Repair.

How are you feeling now? Alleviated? Is tension still mounting?

Fear not, there are two more steps to take before deciding on the best course of action.

The goal of the tool is to focus on your fears, but there's inherent value in reviewing the upside – *conservatively*.

We referenced wanting to hit home runs earlier, but for this exercise, let's consider you only managed a *base hit*.

Tim uses the following prompt:

What might be the benefits of an attempt or partial success?

Perhaps you would learn valuable skills or build up your confidence.

Or maybe you'd make a valuable connection with a future affiliate partner?

Write down at least 5 potential benefits on the left column under "Partial Success Audit."

GROWTH & CHANGE | 305

Lastly, you will consider the cost of inaction, arguably the most important determinant of your next move.

In Tim's version of Fear Setting he breaks down the cost of inaction on a timeline of 6 months, 1 year, and 3 years, but the ANTI-Hustle way is just a tad different.

We like options here, so I find it more impactful for you to decide the timeline for the cost of inaction. If you choose Tim's paradigm, I won't feel slighted in the least.

So if you choose to avoid this action or decision in question, consider the emotional, physical, financial, spiritual, and relational impacts it will have on you – and potentially anyone else affected.

When the pen drops, you may come to the conclusion that inaction is not an option.

You will choose to forge ahead, fears and all, because Fear Setting showed you the pain of staying the same is greater than the pain of change.

And when that happens, you must change.

Or it may conversely confirm your worst fears. It may show you this potential decision or action isn't the right next move.

That's okay too.

Fear Setting is radical in that it's not necessarily a recipe for success but rather a tool to avoid self-destruction and the sinking feeling of impending doom.

And best of all?

Through perspective and trials, you'll soon realize most of the decisions you fear weren't all that scary, to begin with.

TOOLS & RESOURCES

∆∆∆

Access ALL the resources in this chapter and more at:
https://antihustlehandbook.com/toolbox

1. **Kintsugi:** A journal based on the Japanese art and philosophy centered on the notion that your flaws make you stronger and more beautiful
2. **Future Self Journal:** In 6 months from today, how will you have grown personally and professionally?
3. **Mountains You've Climbed:** An inspiring journal prompt to help you realize how far you've come

THE CLOSER
THE REFRAMING TECHNIQUE

△△△

Before you go, really reflect on the progress you've made over the course of just this chapter. Revisit the negative statements from the start of Growth & Change.

Right now is the perfect time to silence the noise and reframe the -isms that got you stuck to begin with.

Trade them out for empowering statements that will help you shift your mindset and strengthen your commitment to a more balanced and intentional life.

	GROWTH & CHANGE: REFRAME	
	From Hustle-ism... *Why am I so stressed all the time?*	**To ANTI-Hustle-ism...** *I'm in my flow state, my comfort zone*
1.	"Look, it's just not going to happen. I tried the best I could, and it is what it is."	
2.	"Ugh! I shouldn't have listened to anyone else — this happens every single time."	
3.	"I'm on the hot mess express, struggle-bussin' my way to the end of the day."	
4.	"Failure isn't an option. I'll figure it out on my own — I have to. I put a lot of money and time into this."	
5.	"I should already be there by now."	

NEXT STEPS

You just ANTI-Hustled your way through Chapter 9!

∆∆∆

REMEMBER

Return to the **Self Assessment**, again and again, to reassess your growth on the ANTI-Hustle journey

Each time, record the date, individual segment scores, and the **Total Balance Factor** to map your progress

ONWARD

1. Go back and check your scores on **Self-Assessment**

2. Identify which segment & chapter you prioritized up next

3. Head there and dig in where it matters most, ANTI-Hustler

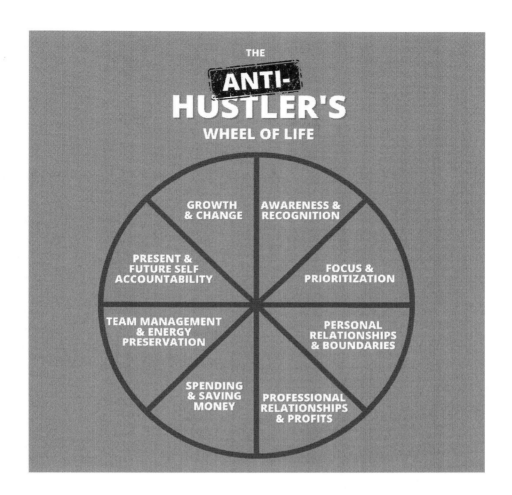

CHAPTER 10
BALANCING NOW & THEN: ANTI-HUSTLE EQUILIBRIUM

FOUNDATION

△△△

The goal of every chapter has been to provide you with actionable steps to beat the hustle and keep ANTI-Hustling your way to greater success.

To do that, you'll have to stay diligent in quieting the noisy Hustle-isms.

Everyone also has their own set of -isms. My parents would always say: "That's such an Alex-ism."

Usually, they're a big part of what we love most about our friends and colleagues.

However, if your -isms happen also to be Hustle-isms, you might find that your ANTI-Hustle work is cut out for you.

Hustle culture is one tough cookie and the Hustle-isms, which are actually negative and limiting self-talk, are incredibly tough habits to break.

Personal "-isms" across the board are often very deeply ingrained, and Hustle-isms are no exception.

Fair warning, it will not be easy to let go of the hustle narrative. No matter the amount of talk and tools and reframing, you might still relapse.

Frustrating, no doubt. Accept this as part of your ANTI-Hustle journey and continue to chip away at striking a balance somewhere between where you were and where you are now.

The ANTI-Hustler Handbook has SO many tools and tricks and tips and anecdotes about trying to achieve equilibrium — in hope that one works for you.

Upset by the idea of a relapse? You might be more upset to learn that you only thought you were winning this whole time.

Is sacrificing everything for nothing in return except an IOU for "getting ahead" in the future, winning now?

I want you to have abundant choices and define and redefine your own success, but maybe be more optimistic — you deserve more. The hard work you put in toward your next move is absolutely valuable, but should always have clear seasons and defined parameters.

To do this, make sure you keep an ear out for those Top Hustle Fails that seem to buzz around no matter what.

Complete the list below by adding in your own **Top Hustle-ism Fails**. Why? To prioritize your journey ahead. To identify your work, look for more options for solutions and to check your progress over time.

Keep this in the forefront: This work won't be hustled.

Change and transformation take time, practice, and patience — *be patient with yourself.*

Top Hustle-ism Fails

1. Life isn't the greatest at this exact moment, but that's all going to change when "x" happens

2. I can do this faster myself

3. My calendar is stacked, I'll have to push this to next week

4. I hate dealing with [client], but I need the money

5. I should already be there by now

6.

7.

8.

9.

10.

MINDSET

△△△

Somewhere on the continuum between hustle culture and the ANTI-Hustle is the concept of having a "beginner's mind."

Neither trek is in any way responsible for the original concept, it's Zen Buddhism that encourages individuals to approach everything with an open and eager mindset, free from preconceptions.

How can this mindset work for both hustlers and the ANTI-Hustle journey? *Is this a hustle hijack?*

Not exactly.

By ditching pre-existing beliefs and judgments, anyone can see things in a new light and get fresh ideas, which ultimately sparks new motivation, amongst other things.

"Beginner's mind" can head up both hustle and ANTI-hustle belief — no hustle heist involved.

Truth be told, everyone has a deep drive to explore alternative perspectives, reevaluate priorities, and create a more fulfilling life.

Here are the major differences that I see between the two:

On getting ahead...

Hustlers believe there is more than one way to get "ahead," but it's still part of a deep, endless grind of "doing whatever it takes because the rent's always due" and sacrificing everything that you're actually working for to get ahead.

&

ANTI-Hustlers believe there is more than one way to define success, so there are more choices for how to be successful.

There's strong pushback against sacrifice, and the focus is on evaluating problems and identifying better solutions for happiness now for Present You and later for Future You.

On re-evaluating priorities...

Hustlers typically seek ways to blend their professional and personal lives, utilizing scheduling and multi-tasking approaches equally for personal and professional relationships.

While the approach is not unnoticed by partners and peers, it still allows for a high level of work without having to reconcile a complete sacrifice of personal obligations.

&

ANTI-hustlers regularly reassess priorities across a personal-professional spectrum.

Doing so ensures they dedicate sufficient time to not only personal relationships but also time allotment for self-care, and leisure activities, instead of solely focusing on professional relationships and work.

On fulfillment...

Hustlers are fulfilled by PLENTY of merchandise — just kidding. That said, fulfillment might be found in reaching ambitious goals, overcoming challenges, and constantly striving for more.

Fulfillment often centers on professional-oriented accomplishments, recognition, and financial rewards as the most significant contributions.

&

ANTI-Hustlers have the same ambitious goals, overcoming challenges and striving for growth apply, but with an evolution of success over time.

Fulfillment might be found in maintaining work-life balance, prioritizing relationships, self-care, and leisure activities alongside professional pursuits.

On both ends of the continuum, adopting a beginner's mind is ideal. The shedding of preconceived notions helps promote adaptability and the resilience necessary for change and transformation.

All of this to say, *the journey isn't linear.*

An abundance of choice also means that it's essential to recognize people can find fulfillment in various ways. Sometimes, just the liminal place between two worlds, combining both hustler and ANTI-hustler approaches is more fulfilling than ever before.

Obviously, taking the next step is ideal, but this may be their most fulfilling experience yet.

Honor that.

Freeing up your head space will help calm and focus your attention on the task at hand. The Brain Dump lets you know that work is here and now, for now. That said, it's time.

The ANTI-Hustle BRAIN DUMP

1. Grab your handy dandy ANTI-Hustler's Companion Handbook at https://antihustlehandbook.com/toolbox
2. Flip to the Brain Dump Prompt for Chapter 10: **What areas of my life could I move toward balance by adopting a beginner's mind?**
3. Put 10 minutes on the clock, and start writing!
4. Do the thing and once the timer dings, continue reading below with newfound clarity.

Hey, *look at you* — more clarity by the minute. By this time, your mindset should be shifting toward a beginner's mind or at least moving toward a more open disposition.

Accept that you might not be ANTI-Hustle yet, and be okay with that. It's something that I am still working on myself. I hope you are, too.

For some people, it takes time, energy, extra effort, and occasionally some sh!tty life lessons to get over the finish line. For other people, the finish line is a consistent measure of improvement, and you never cross it, but you also never kill yourself trying.

Your success is your own. And for success, balance is crucial. But what does that mean, exactly? In physics, **equilibrium is a state of balance.** You can think about the same concept for balancing your life.

Equilibrium isn't always about stillness. It can also be a state of motion where opposing forces cancel each other out.

For example, when a seesaw is evenly balanced, it's in equilibrium. So is a tightrope walker who keeps her center of gravity above the wire.

This is the balance we're looking for — an equilibrium of what feels like all the opposing forces pushing and pulling entrepreneurs.

If that's a hard pass, try thinking of it as The Comfort Zone.

> Remember that ANTI-Hustling is reframing negative attributes into positive affirmations.
>
> The Comfort Zone is a prime example of ANTI-Hustle at its finest.

Painting the Comfort Zone in a negative light is one of the greatest tricks that the Hustle ever pulled.

Just think about it… in the Comfort Zone, you're:

- At mastery level
- Not working hard always
- Doing more of what matters
- Balancing your priorities
- Not in overdrive
- Not subject to death-by-comparison
- Satisfied thanks to choice
- Paying close attention
- Easily saying no
- Focused on your goals
- Staying on your path
- Happy and content

Staying in your comfort zone isn't a bad thing. Comfort isn't a bad thing.

It's also completely fine, normal, and expected to eventually desire - or need - to step out of your comfort zone.

That's where growth happens. It's okay to accept both as true.

ACTION

△△△

Now it's time to take action to quiet the Hustle-isms. Refer back here early and often because the actual action can be trying from time to time.

Try not to forget that doing the right thing is never the wrong thing. To help you remember, one of the best things you can do for yourself is to prioritize yourself. The best way to do that is to rely on the teams of support in your life, whether personal or professional relationships.

I hate to be the bearer of bad news, but those Hustle-isms will always try to sneak back in — *always*. Over the years, I have developed a very advanced technique for combatting this nuisance and maintaining my sanity. I will share it with you right here, right now in hopes it will serve you as it did me.

ANTI-Hustle OMNIPRESENT STATIC SHIELD

Summary

The Omnipresent Static Shield system reduces noise to amplify signal anytime the hustle encroaches.

The process is simple yet effective and can be easily implemented almost anywhere at any time to enact an ANTI-Hustle shield that effectively blocks out the static and harmful Hustle-isms.

Directions

1. Identify where the noise is coming from
2. Determine how loud the noise is
3. Enact the OSS to block the harmful noise
4. Block the noise until you are out of range
5. Keep the shield in good condition

By following the steps in order, you can create an effective shield for a quieter and more peaceful environment that has been known to markedly improve overall well-being and quality of life.

User Manual

Refer to the following diagram taken from the user manual for how best to deal with those irritating Hustle-isms that show up everywhere from gym shirts to burger commercials to kids in the park to water bottles and socks, sheets, movies, and kids' treats for when reframing is good, but it's not quite enough…

THE OMNIPRESENT STATIC SHIELD INTENDED USE OPERATOR MANUAL

1. Hold up both of your hands
2. Close them into fists
3. Extend only your pointer fingers
4. Bend arm at elbow
5. Press a pointer finger in each ear
6. Seal tightly
7. Enjoy the peace and quiet

Seriously, *just shut them out.*

It can be as simple as that. Other times, it might take a little more effort and energy to keep those hustle headaches at bay, but at least you know now.

It's just typical hustle culture BS. Don't buy in.

TOOLS & RESOURCES

ΔΔΔ

Access ALL the resources in this chapter and more at: https://antihustlehandbook.com/toolbox

- Come back here, or to any other chapter, anytime you need to review and revise.

- Take the Self-Assessment again and again.

- Recheck your scores and the areas wherever and whenever you need support.

- Record your progress so you can track your growth. And get ready to be impressed.

- Find an ANTI-Hustle homie. Always be accountable to yourself, both now and then, but linking up with someone else who is on the ANTI-Hustle journey can help you recover from any setbacks and strategize your comeback.

- Hit up the chapters that meet your needs anytime you need them.

NEXT STEPS

Congratulations! You stuck with me through the ANTI-Hustle Handbook Part I & II. Thank you.

∆∆∆

You ANTI-Hustled all the way to the proper end of this book, **The ANTI-Hustler's Handbook.**

If you really went after it and read this Handbook from cover to cover, I applaud you.

If you really went after it and improved your life by just opening the cover of this Handbook, I applaud you.

There is still more ANTI-Hustle goodness to be had if you're up for it…

- Beyond this chapter are more materials in the back of the book: the ANTI-Hustle Toolkit and all the traditional backmatter.
- Remember you also have access to all the online resources and for a more thorough analysis of your journey, look for the ANTI-Hustler Handbook Companion at https://antihustlehandbook.com/toolbox

A few extra things for you when you go…

Here's what I hope you walk away with — there is more than one road to get from where you are right now to where you want to go. And I hope you're on your way after having read this book.

If you're still not quite where you want to be, give yourself a break.

Remember, they did not build Rome in a day. *(Yet, miraculously, the roads they built are still in better shape than most of the highways in Tampa.)* And, even still, the adage says that all roads lead to Rome.

And that's it.

When you have the right tools and the right tactics to get the job done correctly, there's no reason to hustle so hard.

Instead, let systems and processes be guides on your journey. Let them lead so that you can work hard, less.

You can move on to the next leg without ever exhausting yourself; Without ever burning out and losing clarity on what you were working toward in the first place.

Now you know what works for one person, what defines success for another person, doesn't have to be your definition too.

And, in fact, it probably shouldn't be. If it is, at least know that your definition is likely to change to keep Present You and Future You happy and with easy access to more and better choices.

You've got this whole ANTI-Hustle thing down pat, now just go with it.

∆∆∆

Cheers to your success, this is all part of your big victory lap.

I hope it brings you unlimited choices for happiness right now and in the future, ANTI-Hustler.

ΔΔΔ

I can't wait for you to ANTI-Hustle your way to greater success — now and in the future.

— Alex Schlinsky —

ΔΔΔ

— BONUS —
ANTI-HUSTLE TOOLKIT

△△△

Welcome to the ANTI-Hustler's Toolkit!

Here you will find a bevy of tools, resources and templates that will support you on your ANTI-Hustle journey.

You'll find tools here to define your version of success, optimize your relationships, empower your team, create your yellow brick road, measure your happiness, challenge your fears, and so so much more.

Options a plenty.

The tools are organized based on the chapters here in the handbook, plus you can find the templates and swipe files in the Companion Handbook at
https://antihustlehandbook.com/toolbox

Cheers to your success and happiness, *ANTI-Hustler.*

— Alex Schlinsky

Chapter 2 Tools:
Awareness & Recognition

- **The Happiness Quotient:** A test to measure your happiness and fulfillment in your life right now

- **Treasure Map:** Consider this as your personal "Yellow Brick Road." What's the goal we're working towards, and the activities and milestones needed to achieve it?

- **Overwhelm Assessment:** Overwhelm is the outcome of a lack of clarity. Use the assessment to forge your path ahead

- **Mountains You've Climbed:** An inspiring journal prompt to help you realize how far you've come

Chapter 3 Tools:
Focus & Prioritization

- **The Eisenhower Matrix:** How to organize your task list into ensuring you spend your time wisely

- **Daily Focus:** A productivity tool that not only teaches you how to prioritize your tasks daily but also shows you how to batch your tasks appropriately

- **Productivity Strategies:** A Google Doc with 10 strategies, written by the productivity queen herself, my wife Shira

- **5 Questions To Clarity:** A Google Sheet with 5 prompts to help you identify what tasks can be automated, delegated, or outright dumped altogether

Chapter 4 Tools:
Personal Relationships & Boundaries

- **Relationship Life Cycle Audit:** Plotting your relationships into 4 quadrants in order to optimize

- **Love Languages:** Knowing and effectively utilizing Gary Chapman's 5 love languages will deeply impact your relationships

- **Get To, Have To, Want To:** A 3-step journal to help classify your actions in relation to those around you

- **Why Have I Not Done X?:** So often we procrastinate on things we want to do with our loved ones. Why?

Chapter 5 Tools:
Professional Relationships & Profits

- **SWOT:** Evaluating your professional relationships based on Strengths, Weaknesses, Opportunities, and Threats

- **ERAM:** A tool to ensure you and your team are on the same page and what's needed to bolster their effectiveness (See CH. 7)

- **Love Languages:** Knowing and effectively utilizing Gary Chapman's 5 love languages will deeply impact your relationships

- **Enneagram:** A personality system to better understand yourself, your personal relationships, and your professional connections.

Chapter 6 Tools:
Spending & Saving Money

- **Success Calculator:** Defining exactly what is enough money for you to live the life you want

- **Define, Design, Do:** A 3-step process to developing a clear action plan to achieve your personal and professional goals (See CH. 8)

- **Rocketmoney.com:** Formerly Truebill, this app helps better understand your financial health through tracking your expenses

- **Revenue Goal Setting Calculator:** How to achieve your business' financial goals through specific monthly actions & KPIs based on your unique offers and pricing

Chapter 7 Tools:
Team Management & Energy Preservation

- **ERAM:** Ensure you and your team are on the same page and what's needed to bolster their effectiveness

- **Hiring Resources:** There's a slew of recommendations in the ANTI-Hustler Companion Handbook, but here are a few personal favorites: FreeUp, RepStack, Level9 Virtual, Upwork, and Onlinejobs.ph

- **Enneagram:** A personality test to better understand how you and your team members both operate.

- **Job Scorecard & Hiring Templates:** Clearly defined roles, responsibilities, and KPIs help your team succeed.

Chapter 8 Tools:
Present & Future Self Accountability

- **Define, Design, Do:** A 3-step process to developing a clear action plan to achieve your personal and professional goals

- **Spoils Of ~~War~~ Work:** What exactly are you going to do with your business "winnings"?

- **Treasure Map:** Consider this as your personal "Yellow Brick Road." What's the goal we're working towards, and the activities and milestones needed to achieve it?

- **Success Calculator:** How much money is enough money? This calculator will give you the financial clarity you need to live your dream life (See CH. 6)

Chapter 9 Tools:
Growth & Change

- **Fear Setting:** Defining your fears will help you determine what's your next best course of action

- **Kintsugi:** A journal based on the Japanese art and philosophy centered on the notion that your flaws make you stronger and more beautiful

- **Future Self Journal:** In 6 months from today, how will you have grown personally and professionally?

- **Mountains You've Climbed:** How far have you come?

— BONUS —
RECOMMENDED

ΔΔΔ

Wait, do you really need **more**? I thought we talked about this… But I get it, you're on your ANTI-Hustle journey.

In addition to the 40-something tools and 350+ pages, here's some more ANTI-Hustle goodness for you.

You ask I deliver. In no particular order:

- **Prospecting On Demand** - This is my mentorship business for entrepreneurs like you. You should join our community! Yes, shameless self-promotion. Sue me.

- **ANTI-Hustler's Weekly Show** - I host a weekly show in my Facebook group. Come join us!

- **ANTI-Hustler's Weekly Show vault -** You can find the vault at www.alexschlinsky.com/replay-vault

- **7-Figure Sales Savages | Close High-Ticket Clients Daily** - This is my 100% free Facebook Group. Come join us.

- **Follow me on all my socials:** Facebook, TikTok, Instagram, YouTube, LinkedIn, etc. You know the deal. I'm easy to find.

- **Wealth Compounded** - Aba's book on financial planning

- **Essentialism** by Greg McKeown

- **Love Languages** by Gary Chapman

- **4 Hour Work Week, Tools of Titans, Tribe of Mentors** and really anything Tim Ferris has ever written
- **The Five Minute Journal**
- **Getting Things Done** by David Allen
- **HighLevel** - My CRM of choice. Here's my affiliate link: https://bit.ly/ghlalex
- **Business Wars Podcast**
- **RepStack** - A resource for hiring quality talent overseas
- **FreeUp** - A resource for hiring talent stateside
- **InvisiblePPC** - A PPC white-label marketing agency
- **Agency Elevation** - A white-label marketing agency
- **Lofi Girl YouTube Channel** - My playlist for the entirety of writing the ANTI-Hustle Handbook

ACKNOWLEDGEMENTS

△△△

- Thank you to my parents.
- Thank you to my Mom for teaching me that doing the right thing is never the wrong thing.
- Thank you to my Dad for teaching me that success isn't about the money in your bank account but the quality of your relationships.
- Thank you to my brothers Kyle & Dane for constantly inspiring and encouraging me to be the best man I can be.
- Thank you to my wife, Shira.
- Thank you for always believing in me and for making me a better man, husband, and father.
- And most importantly, for truly holding me accountable to the ANTI-Hustle model.
- Thank you to my son, Elie.
- Thank you for giving me the strongest sense of purpose I could ever have, being a Dad is the greatest thing I could ever do.
- Thank you to Jasmine Eastman for your tireless work in helping me share the ANTI-Hustle mantra. This book would not be the same without your insight and dedication.
- Thank you to Christina Hooper for pushing me to write this book. I'll be forever grateful.
- Thank you to William Attaway, the greatest mentor I have ever had.

- Thank you to all the mentors I've had along my journey.
- Thank you to Brian Downard, the best business partner and friend anyone could ever ask for.
- Thank you to the entire Prospecting On Demand team for encouraging me to share my story, holding me accountable, and providing our clients with exceptional service.
- Thank you to the entire Prospecting On Demand community — all past and present members — for being my second family and providing so much enrichment in my life.
- Thank you to Tim Ferris and his Tools For Titans book for the inspiration and courage to write a 'choose your own adventure' book of my own.

AND

- Truly and honestly, I also want to thank R.L. Stine. For every book that you ever wrote, and then let me finish by choosing my own adventure, I am so thankful.

  Not the least of these is the 'Reader Beware: You Choose the Scare' series. Since my foundation for writing was first set in the ever-troubled halls of Madison High, I always knew it would end up being a 'choose your own adventure book' for me (what's up, fellow Goosebumps fans?!).

  It's not just about scaring myself 20 different ways — because moving fast and breaking things will do that to a person too — but it's about the 20 different options, the 20 different choices, the 20 different ways to read the book, the 20 different ways to get what you want out of it on a Tuesday and come back on a Friday and get something different.

ΔΔΔ

Before I go, I have to do a thing. It's part of a process, and it works. I mean, it works until it doesn't, but I like to give it my best every time.

Back to overcoming objections

Take it easy. Rest assured that this might not be a one-book close for you or many other people.

Good news: I have at least a few more up my sleeve, so hang tight. I promise to come back around for you because I know how difficult it can be to shift gears mid-hustle even when you want to so badly.

Change is disruptive. Without the right support, planning, and systems in place, it's really hard. Compound that with how awfully impossible it can be to change — let alone dispel — ingrained beliefs and habits.

Despite the opposition, I believe. I truly believe that the ANTI-hustle philosophy offers a more sustainable and fulfilling path to success. It's one that prioritizes you now and later, it's the fulfillment of goals that you make instead of borrowing, working toward balance rather than early death, and expanding choices as true happiness.

Here I wanted to take a moment to ~~thank the haters~~ express my gratitude to you for even shaking a stick at the ANTI-hustle movement. Time is precious — we all know that. Thank you for taking the time to learn more about it.

Seriously, I understand that this approach is not something that everyone will be ready for this second. Your willingness to explore it nonetheless says more about your commitment to the ANTI-hustle than anything else.

Thank you, again, for following along and digging in, and making headway on your own ANTI-Hustle journey.

Your willingness to engage in the conversation means so much to me professionally and personally — no matter where you stand, this is a dream come true, and thank you for being a part of it.

ΔΔΔ

I appreciate your support & look forward to continuing the dialogue.

Thank you.

— Alex Schlinsky —

ΔΔΔ

ABOUT THE AUTHOR
ALEX SCHLINSKY

△△△

Alex Schlinsky is a long-time entrepreneur and a former hustle-holic, and he knows all too well the toll that constant work and stress can take on one's health, relationships, and overall well-being.

After surviving heart surgery, he realized his obsession with work was not sustainable, and so began his own ANTI-hustle journey.

Through coaching others on business growth, his focus has since shifted from #moremoneymindset to helping entrepreneurs achieve sustainable success without sacrificing the present for the future.

Along the way, Alex founded Prospecting On Demand, a mentorship community that provides entrepreneurs with the tools and support they need to grow their businesses while maintaining a healthy work-life balance.

He also runs a digital marketing agency that serves personal injury attorneys. He's known for his culture of care, strong team, and delivering reliable results.

Alex's client approach is rooted in empathy and continues to grow with a genuine desire to help others.

He understands the challenges that entrepreneurs face and approaches client success with his signature Define, Design, Do model.

Whether you're struggling with the hustle or simply looking for a more sustainable lifestyle design, Alex Schlinsky can help you get from where you are to where you want to go without sacrificing everything important on the way.

The ANTI-hustle isn't just a business strategy, it has the power to transform not only your career but your entire life.

fin

— DO ME A FAVOR? —
Thank You for Reading My Book

△△△

I'd love to hear what you have to say about this book and I need your input to make future books even better.

Please, do me a favor, and take two minutes to leave a helpful review on Amazon letting me know what you thought of this book:

https://antihustlehandbook.com/review

Thank you so much!

— Alex Schlinsky —

Made in the USA
Middletown, DE
25 August 2024